Everyday DOS

**Text and Graphics edited by
Suzanne Weixel**

Trademarks

All terms mentioned in this book that are known to be trademarks or service marks have been appropriately capitalized. Que Corporation cannot attest to the accuracy of this information. Use of a term in this book should not be regarded as affecting the validity of any trademark or service mark.

PC DOS 6 is a trademark of International Business Machines, Corp.

Composed in *Cheltenham* and *MCPdigital* by Que Corporation

Acknowledgments

Thanks to the following folks at Que who got this project off the ground and saw it through to the end: Joe Wikert, Steve Haigh, Bryan Gambrel, and Jodi Jensen.

Thanks also to the following IBMers who helped to ensure the accuracy of the text: Joe Anzalone, Ned Bode, Linda Rogers, Peg Ryan, Sandy Stewart, Diane Walewski, Marie Wolfe, and Laura Zalph.

Publisher: David P. Ewing

Associate Publisher: Rick Ranucci

Operations Manager: Sheila Cunningham

Publishing Plan Manager: Thomas H. Bennett

Marketing Manager: Ray Robinson

Title Manager: Joseph Wikert

Production Editor: Bryan Gambrel

Book Designer: Amy Peppler-Adams

Production Team: Danielle Bird, Julie Brown, Laurie Casey, Brook Farling, Carla Hall-Batton, Michael Hughes, Heather Kaufman, Linda Koopman, Linda Seifert, Sandra Shay, Tina Trettin

Contents at a Glance

Table of Contents

Preface

Welcome to *Everyday DOS* for PC DOS 6.

Although *Everyday DOS* is useful for anyone, it is designed especially for new computer users, casual users, or users with neither the need nor the desire to learn everything there is to know about DOS—people who want to get things done quickly and easily.

If you want to learn more about DOS, IBM provides additional information, both on-line and in book form. Some books are provided with the product, while others can be purchased from IBM separately.

- *Installation Guide*—packaged with DOS 6, this booklet provides step-by-step instructions for installing PC DOS 6.

- *User's Guide*—packaged with DOS 6, this book is for those who want to know even more about DOS. Its primary focus is the DOS utilities.

- *On-line Help*—a built-in feature of DOS 6, it provides you with additional information at the touch of a key.

- *Command Reference and Error Messages*—provided with DOS 6, this book is a printed version of the on-line command reference information.

- *Keyboards and Codepages*—available for purchase separate from DOS 6, this book contains information for those who will be using keyboards other than the U.S. (default) keyboard.

Introduction

This book describes the connection between personal computer hardware and the disk operating system, and explains to beginning users the most frequently used DOS commands from the PC DOS Shell and command line. After you become familiar with DOS's commands and features, you can use the graphics presented here for quick reference.

Making Friends with DOS

DOS is easy! You've heard that statement before. It's the kind of glib remark that might make you wish for an adding machine and ballpoint pen instead of a computer. Maybe you had a personal computer placed on your desk by a manager who "knows you can figure it out."

In a way, that's the worst rub because who wants to admit that you don't know where to begin? After all, your manager might conclude that you are not part of the high-tech generation. He or she might consider you an anachronism in the rapidly changing workplace.

To add to the injury, perhaps everyone's eyes have shifted in your direction, secretly relieved that you—and not they—were chosen for the ordeal. But you are lucky. This book is unlike manuals that usually accompany DOS—those coldly unemotional collections of cryptic commands, disjointed addenda, appendixes, suffixes, prefixes, and file listings.

As a young child, I felt ambivalent about trips to the library. This feeling was odd because I enjoyed reading, and I loved the feel of books in my small hands. Seeing row upon row of file cabinets filled with index cards, however, made my stomach tighten.

In time, I grew accustomed to the patronizing stares of bored librarians and the barbs of superiority from schoolmates. Although I long ago mastered the library system, those wooden cabinets still make me a bit edgy.

Not that the system is incoherent or inconsistent: it isn't. In fact, the logic of the library system is remarkable. Nonetheless, the assumption that a logical system will be easy to learn simply because it is coherent and consistent is the ultimate in callousness.

Every day, thousands of intelligent people scratch their heads and berate themselves. After all, virtually everybody has been inundated by computer advertisements. You see ads in the newspapers, read mailings on sale items, hear about them from friends, and feel guilty about not learning how to use a computer.

Now you have a new computer at your office, or you have decided that a PC will make working at home more efficient. No matter what the reason, you are now face-to-face with DOS.

What Is PC DOS?

By itself, a computer is just a box and a screen. Ultimately, you are faced with the test of bringing it to life. This means mastering the computer's operating system, which for most of us is DOS.

PC DOS (or to most PC users, just DOS) is a tool you use to manage the information your computer stores in disk files. DOS is a collection of programs that forms a foundation for you and your programs to work effectively with your computer. DOS is a set of standard routines that your programs use to access the services of the PC.

No matter what anybody tells you, the letters *D-O-S* do not stand for *Disheartening Obtuse Sadist*. To make the most of your PC, you really have to understand its basics. Understanding DOS is required to enhance the enjoyment and productivity of running your microcomputer.

This book is an introduction to the most widely used disk operating system in the world. You will find that the material presented here is written in a unique manner. You won't be patronized with elementary definitions, and you won't be force-fed a litany of cryptic terms.

What Does This Book Contain?

Learning DOS can be enjoyable. This book is painless and worthwhile reading. Each chapter takes you on a guided tour of a specific part of DOS. You will be introduced to the concept of the DOS Shell and its straightforward, easy-to-use menus. Also, you will be shown how you can type commands that DOS understands by using the command line prompt.

At first you may feel like a spectator, but as you read each chapter, you will find the text fast-moving and the ideas presented in easy-to-understand graphics.

Chapter 1 describes the components of personal computer systems: the display, the keyboard, the system unit, and peripherals. The last part of this chapter traces the way computers handle data.

Chapter 2 introduces you to the look of DOS. In Chapter 3, you will learn about DOS files.

Chapter 4 introduces you to the DOS Shell and teaches you how to operate it, customize it, and use it to find lost files.

Chapter 5 teaches you how to prepare disks so that you can use them and how to protect and maintain them.

Chapter 6 teaches you about directories. You learn how to navigate the tree structure of a disk. You use the Shell's Directory Tree area to visualize the concept of directories.

In Chapter 7, you learn the fundamentals of the E Editor, the built-in PC DOS editor.

And in Chapter 8, you learn how to use the command line to issue commands. This chapter also includes an alphabetical reference of the twenty most useful DOS commands. Use this chapter to find the syntax for commands you want to use from the command line.

Finally, a detailed index helps you quickly find the information you need on a specific topic.

What Hardware Do You Need To Run PC DOS?

The type of computer most likely to use PC DOS is one that is compatible with the International Business Machine Corporation's Personal Computer (IBM PC). COMPAQ, Zenith Data Systems, Gateway, Tandy, Advanced Logic Research, AT&T, AST, EPSON, Wang, NEC, Toshiba, Sharp, Leading Edge, Hewlett-Packard, and many other companies manufacture or market PC DOS-based personal computers.

Your computer should have at least 512 kilobytes (512K) of system random-access memory (RAM), at least one diskette drive, a display (screen), and a keyboard. These suggestions are minimal; most PC DOS PCs sold today exceed these requirements.

You also need at least 4 megabytes of hard disk space to set up DOS 6. To install the optional programs, you need additional hard disk space.

For convenience and processing power, you may want to include a second diskette drive, a hard disk with at least 20 megabytes of storage capacity, a printer, and a color graphics display. You cannot use PC DOS on most computers made by Apple Computer Inc., Commodore (except the new Amiga computers, when equipped with additional hardware), or Atari. These computers use operating systems sometimes referred to as DOS, but their operating systems are not PC DOS compatible.

Conventions Used in This Book

Certain conventions are used throughout the text and graphics of this book to help you better understand the book's subject.

This book uses a variable format to describe command syntax. When you enter a command, you substitute real values for the variable name. Examples present commands you can enter exactly as shown.

DOS commands can have various forms that are correct. For example, the syntax for the DIR command looks like this if you use symbolic names:

DIR *d:filename.ext* /W /P

DIR is the command name. *d:filename.ext* is a variable example of a disk drive name, including its extension, and a filename. A real command would have actual values instead of variables.

Some parts of a command are mandatory—required information needed by PC DOS. Other command parts are optional. In this example, only the DIR is mandatory. The rest of the command, d:filename /W /P, is optional. When you enter only the mandatory command elements, DOS in many cases uses values already established for the optional parts.

You can type upper- or lowercase letters in commands. DOS reads both as uppercase letters. You must type syntax samples shown in this book letter-for-letter, but you can ignore case. Items shown in lowercase letters are variables. You type the appropriate information for the items shown in lowercase letters.

In the preceding example, the lowercase *d:* identifies the disk drive the command will use for its action. Replace *d:* with A:, B:, or C:. The *filename.ext* stands for the name of a file, including its extension.

Spaces separate some parts of the command line. The slash separates other parts. The separators, or delimiters, are important to DOS because they help DOS break apart the command. For example, typing **DIR A:** is correct, but **DIRA:** is not.

In the numbered steps, the text you must type is displayed in **boldface** and keys are shown as they appear on the keyboard, such as Ctrl or F7. Screen messages appear in this special monospaced typeface. Callouts emphasize some of the more important areas of the graphics illustrations.

This book is your guide to becoming comfortable using DOS on your personal computer.

Learning About Your Computer

1

Have you ever wondered why our society has emotional attachments for some machines, but not for others? We love our automobiles, for example, but we don't feel that way about our refrigerators, garbage disposals, or lawn mowers.

This attachment to cars comes from our capacity to develop a very interactive relationship with a mechanical beast. We are social creatures, and not many mechanical contraptions supply us with that give-and-take we seem to need, which may be why we have such love affairs with contraptions that do.

For some people, a personal computer is another machine that provides an abundance of emotional "bang for the buck." Other people, however, may feel disappointment with their first computer purchase. It may appear to be little more than a big, dumb box. If not for the fact that most people must use a personal computer for business, they may have preferred to buy a new television set.

Although you may be anxious about getting started, once you understand something about how the computer works, you will feel a good deal better about learn-ing to use it. This chapter provides a quick, but illuminating, lesson about how personal computers work. Learning about the personal computer, its components, and how all the parts work together is like learning new car controls: displays and keyboards (dashboards), the CPU (engine control unit), peripherals (tires), and disk drives (the cassette player).

1

Does a computer take you from zero to sixty in six seconds? Even faster: it takes you close to the speed of light. Computers may not yet turn you into an Indy 500 car driver, but you will be able to participate in a drama of your own making.

This chapter explains the components that have become a standard for the IBM PC and compatibles. Do you need to remember every term you read? Not unless you are a college student preparing for a final exam. Nevertheless, this chapter's design will help you enjoy working with your new computer. After all, knowing where the oil goes in your car is always useful. And as cars have their own terminology, so does the personal computer.

Every term defined here is rooted in the English language. These terms are no more mysterious than terms such as *dashboard, acceleration, mileage, pause,* or *reverse.* Computer terms are simple to remember and impressive to use at the office. Knowing them may even get you a raise.

Key Terms Used in This Chapter	
CPU	Stands for central processing unit: the processor in which the actual computing takes place. It is the brain of the computer.
Display	The screen or monitor.
Peripheral	Any device, aside from the computer itself, that permits you to do something or shows the results. A good example of a peripheral is your printer.
Disk	A plastic or metal platter used to store files. A disk drive records and reads back information on disks. Disks come in two basic sizes and function like the cassettes you place in your tape recorder. The main difference between disks and cassettes is that disks resemble small LP records. Like the arm of a phonograph, the read/write head swings into position over the spinning disk to make data retrieval quick and simple. The disk drive head can swing right to the data you need.

1

Modem	A device for exchanging data between computers through standard telephone lines. A modem is similar to your telephone handset—just remember that a computer does not have mechanical hands, vocal cords, or ears. All information transfers via computer-generated audio signals.
Input	Any data given to a computer.
Output	Any data transmitted by a computer.
Bit	A binary digit. The smallest discrete representation of a value a computer can manipulate. A computer thinks only in numbers. Several numbers make up a character, such as a word or letter. In short, bits are similar to the dot/dash concept used in Morse code.
Byte	A collection of eight bits that a computer usually stores and manipulates as a full character (letter, number, or symbol). A byte is a character identified by a sequence of numbers.
K (kilobyte)	1,024 bytes, used to show size or capacity in computer systems. Technically, the term *kilo* means thousand, but you must allow the computer revolution its poetic license.
M (megabyte)	1,024 kilobytes.
Data	A broad term meaning words, numbers, symbols, graphics, or sounds. Data is any information stored in computer byte form.
File	A named group of data in electronic form. In word processing, a file can be a letter to a friend. In a database system, a file can be a name-and-address telephone listing.
Network	Two or more computers linked together by cables. They can share data, files, and peripherals.

1 Computer Technology Defined

Computers used to be large, expensive machines generally unavailable to individual users. Although the rich could afford them, not many people wanted to fill three rooms of their homes with energy-guzzling electronics that served no practical purpose.

Advances in computer technology led to the engineering of smaller computer parts called *integrated circuits,* more commonly known as *chips.* The actual processing in a personal computer takes place on one of these chips, called the *microprocessor.* The newer, high-capacity chips meant a savings in both space and energy. The ultimate product of chip technology is the *microcomputer* as exemplified by your personal computer.

In 1981, International Business Machines (IBM) introduced the IBM Personal Computer, or PC. The IBM PC was the first personal computer to earn the respect of the business community. As a leader in the large business computer market, IBM was uniquely positioned to make the PC today's standard in home and business computing. The arrival of the Personal Computer worked out well. IBM created both a market for PCs and a standard upon which other firms have built.

Although the Apple II and Macintosh are also personal computers, the term *PC* has come to mean computers that are made by IBM and other manufacturers and that run PC DOS, or a compatible operating system. Originally, PCs by other manufacturers were called *compatibles,* but were only partially compatible with the IBM PC. Today, these personal computers are often called *clones* and, if well-made, operate virtually the same as the equivalent IBM models.

Today, rapid technological developments in newly created companies are raising microcomputer technology to new heights. Never before could you purchase so much computing power at such a reasonable price.

Components of Computer Systems

A computer system is composed of hardware parts that exist in a variety of configurations. All PC DOS computers operate in essentially the same manner. Engineers base the size of the computer more on human physiology than on anything else. Designers developed the standard model to be large enough to contain disk drives and other devices. The portable, on the other hand, is small and light, perfect for computing while on the road.

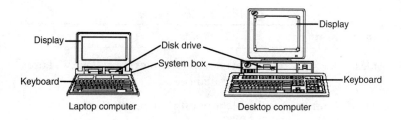

Laptop computer   Desktop computer

Personal computer systems based on the IBM PC are functionally the same, despite the wide variety of configurations available. As long as you have the main components, the shape and size of your computer matters very little. For example, you can find equally powerful machines in the traditional desktop configuration, in floor models, in portable laptop models, or in compact, lunch box-sized computers. The wide variety of PC software operates equally well in any of these cosmetic configurations.

Hardware and software make up the two main segments of a computer system. Both segments must be present for a computer to work. Many texts waste several pages supplying complicated definitions for terms that are simple, but this book won't.

Hardware refers to the physical machine and its peripherals—electronics and moving parts of metal and plastic. A VCR, television, tape deck, CD player, and turntable are everyday examples of hardware.

Software encompasses the program and data files created, stored, and run by your PC. These records are the equivalent of text books, novels, newspapers, and videotapes. Table 1.1 illustrates the variety of software available for a computer.

Table 1.1
Computer Software

Type of software	*Examples*
Operating systems	PC DOS; OS/2; UNIX
Databases	dBASE IV; Paradox; PC-FILE
Spreadsheets	Lotus 1-2-3; Excel; Quattro Pro
Word processors	WordPerfect; Microsoft Word; PC-WRITE
Utilities	Fastback Plus; PC Tools Deluxe; SideKick

continues

11

1

Table 1.1 *(Continued)*

Type of software	*Examples*
Graphics	Harvard Graphics; CorelDRAW; Lotus Freelance
Integrated programs	Symphony; Microsoft Works; Q&A
Games	Flight Simulator; Tetris; SimCity
Home finance	Quicken; Managing Your Money
Desktop publishing	First Publisher; Ventura Publisher; PageMaker

The operating system provides the working base for all other programs by creating a uniform means for programs to gain access to the full resources of the hardware. Operating systems that help programs access disks are called *disk operating systems,* or DOS.

This book covers the PC DOS operating system for IBM PC compatibles. The IBM versions of DOS and the various versions of Microsoft Corporation's DOS are highly compatible and very similar.

Text and Graphics Displays

The video *display* (also called the *monitor* or *screen*) describes the part of the computer's hardware that produces visual images. To date, the cathode ray tube (CRT) type of monitor, which operates on the same principle as a television set, provides the most crisp, easily read image.

On the display, a blinking symbol (box, underscore, or other character) shows where the next character will appear. This symbol is the cursor.

```
C:\>dir /w

 Volume in drive C is IBMDOS_6
 Volume Serial Number is 1A83-720A
 Directory of C:\

COMMAND.COM    [DOS]          WINA20.386     [UTILS]        CONFIG.OLD
AUTOEXEC.OLD   [DATA]         [WINDOWS]      [XYWRITE]      CONFIG.WRD
AUTOEXEC.WRD   [WORD]         CONFIG.SYS     AUTOEXEC.BAT   MOUSE.SYS
[PC-TALK]
         16 file(s)        97533 bytes
                        66408448 bytes free

C:\>_
```

Personal computers are *interactive.* Interactive means that the PC reacts to any action you take and shows the results on the computer display screen. The video display is the normal, or *default,* location the computer uses to communicate with you.

Manufacturers also incorporate other types of technology into computer displays. For example, to build flatter displays, manufacturers use a technology known as *gas plasma.* Gas plasma displays produce an orange color against a dark background. This type of display is found primarily in portable computers, where a TV-type display would be heavy and cumbersome.

Another technology adapted to computer displays is liquid crystal. *Liquid crystal displays* (LCDs) work on the same principle as today's digital watch displays. Most LCDs produce dark characters against a lighter background. LCDs work well in brightly lit rooms, because the light striking the display increases the contrast of the display image. Some LCDs also use a backlight to increase the display's contrast. This type of display appears primarily on laptop computers.

Regardless of the display type, all computer screens take electrical signals and translate them into patterns of tiny dots, or *pixels.* Pixel is an acronym coined from the phrase *picture element.* You can recognize pixels as characters or figures. The more pixels a display contains, the sharper the visual image. The number of pixels in the image multiplied by the number of lines on the display determines the image's *resolution.*

Image Resolution   *Image Resolution*

The higher-resolution image (left) uses four times as many pixels as the low-resolution image (right).

The resolution of the visual image is a function of both the display and the *display adapter.* The display adapter controls the computer display. In some PCs, the display circuitry is a part of the motherboard (see this chapter's section "The System Unit and Peripherals"). The display adapter also can reside on a separate board that fits into a slot in the computer. The display adapter can be a monochrome display adapter (MDA), Hercules monochrome graphics adapter (MGA), color graphics adapter (CGA), enhanced graphics

1

adapter (EGA), video graphics array adapter (VGA), extended graphics array adapter (XGA), super video graphics array adapter (SVGA), or a less common display adapter.

Text Display

When you see letters, numbers, or punctuation on your display, you recognize these images as text. This text comes from your computer's memory where the text has been stored under the standard that most computers recognize, the *American Standard Code for Information Interchange (ASCII).* Text displays and text display adapters can display only text characters. They cannot display graphics characters.

Each ASCII code represents a letter or a symbol. These codes are sent to the display adapter so that you can see the characters on-screen. The display adapter has a built-in electronic table from which the adapter can take the correct pixel pattern for any letter, number, or punctuation symbol.

Although 128 standard ASCII codes exist, a single computer character can contain 256 different codes. The upper codes are known as IBM *extended ASCII codes.* These additional codes are used for patterns of foreign language letters, mathematical symbols, lines, corners, and special images, such as musical notes.

If a program needs to display a pixel or pattern of pixels not included in the ASCII-to-pixel table, you are out of luck. Text displays and text display adapters cannot generate graphics. Of the various display adapters available, only the monochrome display adapter (MDA) is a text-only display adapter. Because so much software today is graphically oriented, virtually all personal computers sold today have graphics displays.

Graphics Display

Graphics displays can produce any pixel or pattern of pixels. This type of display enables you to view, on-screen, complex figures with curves and fine detail. The computers work harder to create graphics images than text images, however, because images are "painted" on the screen with pixels. To display the correct point on-screen, the display adapter must find the screen coordinate points for each pixel. Unlike the ASCII codes in text mode, no table of predetermined pixels exists for graphics mode.

Graphics displays differ in the number of pixels available. The greater the number of pixels, the finer the detail of the display. Each pixel contains characteristics that describe to the graphics adapter what the color or intensity of the pixel should be. The greater the number of colors and intensities, the more storage space you need in memory. Graphics adapters offer varying combinations of pixel density, number of colors, and intensity.

Table 1.2 lists the most common display adapters, showing the maximum resolution and the colors available with each type of display adapter.

Table 1.2
Resolution and Colors for Display Adapters

Adapter Type	Graphics Mode	Pixel Resolution	Colors Available
CGA	Medium resolution	320 x 200	4
CGA	High resolution	640 x 200	2
EGA	CGA high resolution	640 x 200	16
EGA	EGA high resolution	640 x 350	16
MGA	Monochrome graphics	720 x 348	2
MDA	Text characters only	80 x 25	2
VGA	Monochrome	640 x 480	2
VGA	VGA high resolution	640 x 480	16
VGA	VGA medium resolution	320 x 200	256
Super VGA	Super VGA	800 x 600	256
Super VGA	1024 Super VGA	1024 x 768	256
XGA	Standard mode	1024 x 768	256
XGA	16-bit color	640 x 480	65,536

The number of colors available on the display depends on the program you are using and the amount of memory on the adapter. For example, a Super VGA adapter with 512K of video memory can display 256 colors, but the software might display only 16 colors. A Super VGA adapter with 256K of video memory can display only 16 colors, even if the software can display 256 colors.

1   Keyboards

The keyboard is the most basic way to enter information into the computer. The computer then converts every character you type into code the machine can understand. The keyboard is therefore an *input device.*

Like a typewriter, a computer keyboard contains all the letters of the alphabet. The numbers, symbols, and punctuation characters are virtually the same. The computer keyboard has the familiar QWERTY layout. The term *QWERTY* comes from the letters found on the left side of the top row of character keys on a standard typewriter. However, a computer keyboard differs from a typewriter keyboard in several important ways.

The most notable differences of the computer keyboard are the extra keys that do not appear on a typewriter. These keys and their standard functions are described in Table 1.3. Some of these keys have different functions when used with different programs. Also, depending on the type of computer and keyboard you use, you will see 10 or 12 special *function keys.*

Table 1.3
Special Keys on the Computer Keyboard

Key	*Name*	*Function*
⏎Enter	Enter	Signals the computer to respond to the commands you type. Also functions as a carriage return in programs that simulate the operation of a typewriter.
↑ ↓ ← →	Cursor keys	Changes the cursor location on-screen. Included are the arrow, PgUp, PgDn, Home, and End keys.
←Backspace	Backspace	Moves the cursor backward one space at a time, deleting any character in that space.
Del	Delete	Deletes, or erases, any character at the location of the cursor.
Ins	Insert	Inserts any character at the location of the cursor.

1

Key	Name	Function
⟨⇧Shift⟩	Shift	Capitalizes letters when you hold down Shift as you press another letter key. When pressed in combination with another key, Shift can change the standard function of that key.
⟨Caps Lock⟩	Caps Lock	Enables you to enter all capital letters when the key is pressed down in the locked position. Caps Lock doesn't shift the numbered keys, however. To release Caps Lock, press the key again.
⟨Ctrl⟩	Control	Changes the standard function of a key when pressed in combination with another key.
⟨Alt⟩	Alternate	Changes the standard function of a key when pressed in combination with another key.
⟨Esc⟩	Escape	Enables you to escape from a current operation to a previous one in some situations. Sometimes Esc has no effect on the current operation.
⟨Num Lock⟩	Number Lock	Changes the numeric keypad from cursor-movement to numeric-function mode.
⟨PrtSc⟩	Print Screen	Sends the displayed characters to the printer. This key is provided on Enhanced keyboards.
⟨Scroll Lock⟩	Scroll Lock	Locks the scrolling function to the cursor-movement keys so that they scroll the screen instead of moving the cursor.

continues

1

Table 1.3 *(Continued)*

Key	Name	Function
[Pause]	Pause	Suspends display activity until you press another key. (Not provided with standard keyboards.)
[Break]	Break	Stops a program in progress from running.
[7] [8] [9] [4] [5] [6] [1] [2] [3] [0] [.]	Numeric keypad	A cluster of keys to the right of the standard keyboard. The keypad includes numbered keys from 0 to 9 as well as cursor-movement keys and other special keys.

Many of the function keys are designed for use in combination with other keys (see Table 1.4). For example, holding down the Ctrl key as you press the Print Screen key causes DOS to continuously print what you type. Pressing Ctrl and Print Screen a second time turns off the printing. The Break key is not a separate key. With some keyboards, pressing the Ctrl and Scroll Lock keys together causes a break. With other keyboards, pressing the Ctrl and Pause keys together causes a break.

Table 1.4
DOS Key Combinations

Key Combination	Function
[Ctrl]-[S]	Freezes the display. Pressing any other key restarts the display.
[Ctrl]-[PrtSc]	Sends lines to both the screen and the printer. Pressing this sequence a second time turns off this function.
[Ctrl]-[C] or [Ctrl]-[Break]	Stops a program that is active.
[Ctrl]-[Alt]-[Del]	Restarts PC DOS (system reset).

The function keys are shortcuts or command keys. Not all programs use these keys, and some programs use only a few of them. When used, however, these keys automatically carry out certain operations for you. For example, programs often use the F1 key for *on-line help.* On-line help displays instructions to help you understand a particular operation. The PC DOS Shell uses the F3 key to cancel the Shell. The F10 key activates the menu.

The original standard keyboard contains the function keys F1 through F10 on the left side. The standard Extended keyboard offers keys F1 through F12, which are located across the top of the standard keyboard. Some users find that the location of the function keys on the Extended keyboard isn't as convenient. On the other hand, many users find the separate cursor-control keypad a real advantage.

AT and Enhanced Keyboards

Many early PC-compatible computers use a standard keyboard design similar to that of the IBM PC. Other machines use a Personal Computer AT-style keyboard. The IBM PS/2 computers and almost all other personal computers today use a 101-key Enhanced keyboard. Some users prefer the layout of the standard keyboard, and others prefer the Enhanced keyboard.

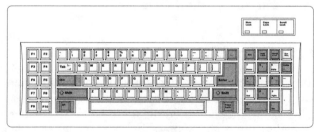

AT keyboard

You can determine whether your computer has a standard keyboard, a Personal Computer AT-style keyboard, or an Enhanced keyboard. You find certain keys only on specific keyboards. For example, you find separate PrtSc and Pause keys only on the Enhanced keyboard. You can, however, simulate these keys by using a combination of keys on the standard keyboard.

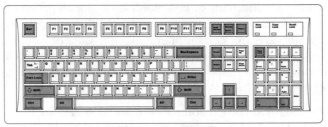

Enhanced keyboard

Special Keyboards

Some new keyboards try to provide the advantages of both the older and the newer keyboards. Such keyboards enable you to change key caps and switch key definitions for the Caps Lock, Ctrl, Esc, and tilde (~) keys. Some keyboards provide the enhanced layout, but locate the function keys on the left side of the keyboard instead of at the top.

Northgate Computer Systems, for example, offers keyboards with the separate cursor keys arranged exactly the same as they are on the numeric keyboard. This arrangement makes the cursor keys easier to use with most software. One keyboard model has a set of functions keys across the top and a second set on the left so that you can choose which set to use.

Keyboards for Portables

Small "lunch box" and laptop portable computers employ nonstandard keyboards, usually to conserve space. A *space-saver keyboard* is small enough to fit in a portable computer, but often the trade-off for its smaller size is fewer keys and less functionality. A few of these computers have so little keyboard space that you may need to add an external numeric keypad for software that manipulates numbers.

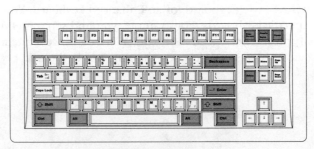

Space-saver keyboard

The System Unit and Peripherals

Industry engineers designed the standard desktop PC around a box-shaped cabinet that connects to all other parts of the computer. This box is called the *system unit*, which includes disk drives and disks. Any devices attached to the system unit are *peripherals*. The system unit and the peripherals complete the hardware portion of the computer system.

The System Unit

The system unit houses all but a few parts of a PC. Included are various circuit boards, the disk drives, a power supply, and even a small speaker.

The system units on today's PCs come in many variations of the original design. Desktop models are smaller to conserve desk space. Larger models with room for larger, multiple hard disks and other peripherals often use a floor-standing tower design that requires no desk space at all.

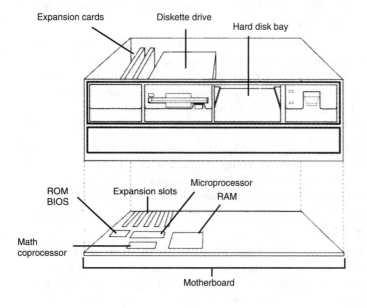

A hypothetical system unit, showing the placement of the hard and diskette drives and the system board, also called the motherboard.

The *motherboard* holds the main electronic components of the computer. The microprocessor, the chips that support it, and various other circuits are the primary parts on the motherboard. The motherboard usually contains electrical sockets in which you can plug various adapter circuit boards. These electrical sockets are called *expansion slots*.

Chips that provide the computer with its memory are located on the mother-board. You can plug additional memory adapter cards into an available expansion slot to increase the system's memory. The number of available expansion slots varies with each PC builder. Most motherboards have a socket for a *math coprocessor*. Math coprocessors help speed up programs that manipulate large volumes of graphics or math equations. Spreadsheet programs and desktop publishing software, for example, benefit from the addition of a math coprocessor chip.

Disk Drives and Disks

Disk drives are complex mechanisms that carry out a fairly simple function: they rotate *disks,* which are circular platters or pieces of plastic that have magnetized surfaces. As the disk rotates, the drive converts electrical signals from the computer and places the information into or retrieves information from magnetic fields on the disk. The storage process is called *writing* data to the disk. Disk drives also recover, or *read,* magnetically stored data and present it to the computer as electrical signals. Magnetically stored data is not lost when you turn off the computer.

The components of a disk drive are similar to those of a phonograph or a CD player. The disk, like a record, rotates. A positioner arm, like a tone arm, moves across the radius of the disk. A head, like a pickup cartridge, translates information into electrical signals. Unlike a record, the disk's surface does not have spiral grooves. The disk's surface is recorded in magnetic, concentric rings, or tracks. The tighter these tracks are packed on the disk, the greater the storage capacity of the disk.

Two types of disks are available, which come in a variety of data storage capacities. Disks can be *diskettes* or *hard disks*. Diskettes are removable, flexible, slower, and of a lower capacity than hard disks. Hard disks, also called *fixed* disks, are usually high-capacity rigid platters that you cannot remove—unlike diskettes.

When a computer writes to the disk, it stores groups of data that the operating system identifies as *files*. You can tell that a drive is reading or writing a diskette when the small light on the front of the disk drive glows. You should never open a drive door or eject a disk until the light goes out, unless the computer specifically instructs you to do so.

When a hard drive is reading or writing data, a light may glow on the front of the drive or there may be a separate disk-drive light on the front of the system unit.

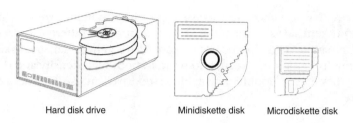

Hard disk drive   Minidiskette disk   Microdiskette disk

Hard disks are sealed inside the hard disk drive. Diskettes are encased in flexible 5 ¼-inch jackets or in rigid 3 ½-inch jackets.

Diskettes

Diskettes store from 360K to 2.88M bytes of data and come in two common sizes. Originally, the 5 ¼-inch diskettes were called *minidiskettes* to distinguish them from the 8-inch disks used on very early personal computers. The 3 ½-inch diskettes are sometimes called *microdiskettes*. The measurement refers to the size of the disk's jacket. Unless size is important, this book simply refers to both disk types as *diskettes*.

In almost all cases, the disk drive uses both sides of a disk for encoding information; therefore, the disk drives and the diskettes are called *double-sided*.

A drive can handle only one size diskette. You cannot read a 5 ¼-inch diskette in a 3 ½-inch diskette drive or vice versa. Table 1.5 shows a number of different diskette capacities. Only the most common diskette types are listed. The disk capacities are in kilobytes (K) or megabytes (M).

Table 1.5
Common Diskette Types

Diskette Type	Capacity
5 ¼-inch	
Double-density	360K
High-density	1.2M
3 ½-inch	
Double-density	720K
High-density	1.44M
	2.88M

1

Make sure that you know your drive's specification before you buy or inter-change diskettes. Diskettes of the same size but with different capacities can be incompatible with a particular diskette drive. A high-density diskette drive, for example, can format, read, and write to both high-density and double-density diskettes. A double-density diskette drive can use only double-density diskettes.

Hard Disks

Hard disks often consist of multiple, rigid-disk platters. Each side of each platter has a separate head. The platters spin at 3,600 RPM, much faster than a diskette drive spins. As the platters spin within the drive, the head positioners make small, precise movements above the tracks of the disk. Because of this precision, hard disks can store large quantities of data—from 10M to hundreds of megabytes. Hard disks are reasonably rugged devices. Factory sealing prevents contamination of the housing. With proper care, hard disks can deliver years of trouble-free service.

Peripherals

Besides the display, keyboard, and disk drives, a variety of peripherals can be useful to you. Peripherals such as a mouse, printer, modem, joystick, digitizer, and a microphone enable you to communicate with your computer easily. For example, using a mouse with a modern computer program—such as a desk-top publishing package—takes best advantage of the program's features.

A mouse is a com-puter pointing device whose shape vaguely resembles that of a real mouse. You use a mouse with graphics programs and modern graphical interfaces such as the DOS Shell.

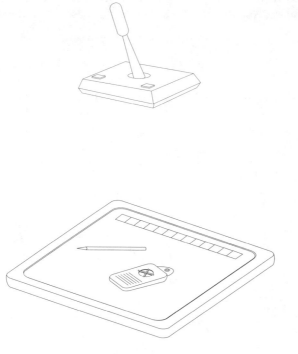

A joystick is a popular peripheral in games and is used to enter information into the computer. Sometimes joysticks are used in place of keyboard operations.

For many users, a digitizer tablet feels more natural than using a mouse. When a digitizer's "puck" moves across the tablet, that motion is displayed on-screen. It is used most often in high-end graphics and computer-aided design (CAD) programs.

New products, such as IBM VoiceType, allow you to run programs by speaking to your computer through an attached microphone, instead of using a keyboard.

The Mouse

The mouse is a pointing device that you move on the surface of your work space and that causes the computer to correlate this movement to the display. The mouse is shaped to fit comfortably under your hand. The contour of the mouse and the cable that trails from the unit give the vague appearance of a mouse sitting on the table. The mouse has two or three buttons that rest beneath the fingers of your hand.

1

You use the mouse to move a *mouse pointer* to make menu selections, draw with graphics programs, move the keyboard cursor swiftly, and select sections of your work to manipulate. Not all software supports a mouse, but many popular programs do.

Printers

Printers accept signals (*input*) from the CPU and convert those signals to characters (*output*), usually imprinted on paper. You can classify printers in the following ways:

- How they receive input from the computer
- How they produce output

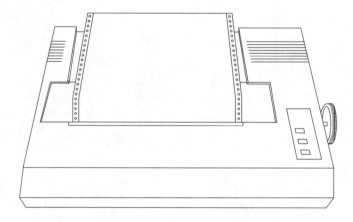

A printer accepts data from the computer and renders it as text and images on paper.

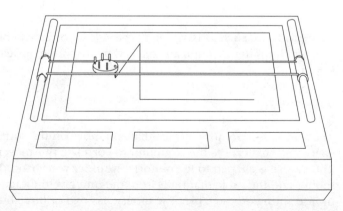

A plotter lets you draw with the computer. Unlike the printer, a plotter draws up and down as well as back and forth.

You connect printers to the system unit through a *port*. A port is an electrical doorway through which data flows between the system unit and an outside peripheral. A port has its own expansion adapter or shares an expansion adapter with other ports or circuits, such as a multifunction card.

The terms *parallel* and *serial* describe two types of ports that send output from personal computers to printers. A parallel port continuously sends all the bits of data synchronously, through separate wires in the cable, one byte (character) at a time. Parallel printer connections are more common than serial connections. A serial port delivers the bits of data, one bit after another, in single-file fashion. Although sending one complete byte by using serial communications takes longer, serial ports require fewer wires in the cable. Serial printers also can communicate with the port over longer distances than parallel printers.

All printers have the job of putting their output onto paper. This output often is text, but it also can be graphics images. Four major classifications of printers exist: *dot-matrix, laser, inkjet,* and *daisywheel.* Each printer type produces characters in unique ways. Printers usually are rated by their printing speed and the quality of the finished print. Some printers print by using all the addressable points on the screen, much as a graphics display adapter does. Some printers even produce color prints.

The most common printer, the dot-matrix, uses a print head that contains a row of pins or wires to produce the characters. A motor moves the print head horizontally across the paper. As the print head moves, a vertical slice of each character forms as the printer's controlling circuits fire the proper pins. The wires press corresponding small dots of the ribbon against the paper, leaving an inked dot impression. After several tiny horizontal steps, the print head leaves the dot image of a complete character. The process continues for each character on the line. Dot-matrix printers are inexpensive. With the print quality close to that of a typewriter, this type of printer is commonly used for internal reports.

Laser printers use a technology that closely resembles that of photocopying. Instead of a light-sensitive drum picking up the image of an original, the drum is painted with the light of a laser diode. The image on the drum transfers to the paper in a high dot density output. With high dot density, the printed characters look fully formed. Laser printers also can produce graphics image output. The high-quality text and graphics combination is useful for desktop publishing as well as general business correspondence.

The inkjet printer literally sprays words and graphics on a page in near silence. Moderately priced, the print quality rivals that of a laser printer, and of all the printers, only a laser printer is faster and sharper than this high-resolution printer.

1

The daisywheel printer steps, or moves incrementally, a print head across the page and produces a complete character for each step. The characters of the alphabet are arranged at the ends of "petals" that resemble spokes on a wheel. The visual effect of this wheel is similar to a daisy's petals arranged around the flower head. Because the daisywheel prints fully-formed characters, the quality of daisywheel printing is about the same as a typewriter. Daisywheel printers are far slower than the other printers and are virtually obsolete.

Modems

A modem is a peripheral that helps your PC communicate with other computers over standard telephone lines. Modems are serial communications peripherals. They send or receive characters or data one bit at a time. Most modems communicate with other modems at speeds from 300 to 9600 bits per second (bps), and speeds up to 19,200 bps are not unusual. The most common speed for modems, however, is 2400 bps. Modems need special communications software to coordinate data exchanges with other modems.

You use a modem to send or receive files to another computer, to use a computerized *bulletin board system* (BBS), or to access an on-line service such as Prodigy or CompuServe.

A modem
transfers signals
between
computers by
using telephone
lines.

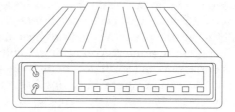

How Computers Work with Data

Now that you have learned about the essential parts of the computer system, you are ready for an overview of how all these parts carry out the job of computing. The world inside a computer is a strange place. Fortunately, you do not have to know the details of a computer's operation to produce finished work. If you explore a little bit, however, you will adjust more quickly to using your computer.

Computers perform many useful tasks by accepting data as input, processing it, and releasing it as output. Data is information. It can be a set of numbers, a memo, an arrow key that moves a game symbol, or anything you can imagine.

The computer translates input into electrical signals that move through a set of electronic controls. Output can be thought of in four ways:

- As characters the computer displays on-screen
- As signals the computer holds in its memory
- As codes stored magnetically on disk
- As permanent images and graphics printed on paper

Computers receive and send output in the form of electrical signals. These signals are stable in two states: on and off. Think of these states as you would electricity to a light switch that you can turn on and off. Computers contain millions of electronic switches that can be either on or off. All input and output follows this two-state principle.

Binary, the computer name for the two-state principle, consists of signals that make up true computer language. Computers interpret data as two binary digits, or *bits*—0 and 1. For convenience, computers group eight bits together. This eight-bit grouping, or *byte,* is sometimes packaged in two-, four-, or eight-byte packages when the computer moves information internally.

Computers move bits and bytes across electrical highways called *buses.* Normally, the computer contains three buses: the *control bus,* the *data bus,* and the *address bus.* The microprocessor connects to all three buses and supervises their activity. The CPU uses the data bus to determine what the data should be, the control bus to confirm how the electrical operations should proceed, and the address bus to determine where the data is to be positioned in memory.

Because the microprocessor can call on this memory at any address and in any order, it is called *random-access memory,* or *RAM.* The CPU reads and activates program instructions held in RAM. Resulting computations are stored in RAM.

Some computer information is permanent. This permanent memory, called *read-only memory* (or *ROM*), is useful for holding unalterable instructions in the computer system.

1

Displaying a word on a computer screen seems simple: you just press keys. However, each time you enter a character, the computer performs a complex series of steps.

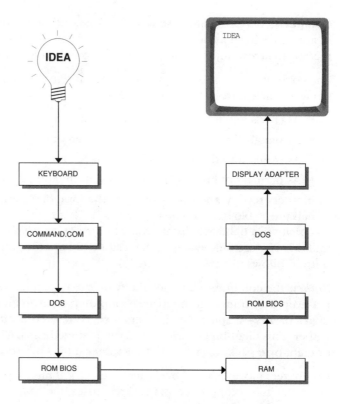

The microprocessor depends on you to give it instructions in the form of a *program.* A program is a set of binary-coded instructions that produce a desired result. The microprocessor decodes the binary information and carries out the instruction from the program.

You can start from scratch and type programs or data into the computer every time you turn on the power. Of course, you don't want to do that if you don't have to. The good news is that the computer stores both instructions and start-up data, usually on a disk. Disks store data in binary form in *files.* To the computer, a file is just a collection of bytes identified by a unique name. This collection of bytes can be a memo, a word processing program, or some other program. A file's function is to hold binary data or programs safely until you type a command from the keyboard to direct the microprocessor to call for that data or program file. When the call comes, the drive reads the file and writes its contents into RAM.

Stand-Alone versus Networked PCs

Until the mid 1980s, most personal computers were *desktop,* or *stand-alone* models, which meant that the software and hardware that comprised each PC was designed for a single user. Today PCs in a corporate environment often are linked by cables into *networks* or *workgroups.* PCs on a network can share data, applications, and peripherals. For a business, that capability translates into increased productivity; it ensures that employees are using the same tools and can communicate easily, and it decreases spending because fewer peripherals and software programs are purchased.

In a PC network, each user still has a PC on his or her desktop. To the individual user, the PC looks and acts like a stand-alone system; however, it may not have all the components of a stand-alone, such as disk drives. The PCs are managed by a more powerful PC called a *server.* The server stores the software and controls the data input and output.

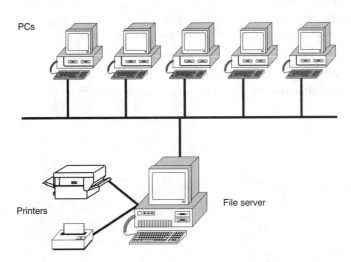

PCs

Printers

File server

Networked PCs can share files, applications, and peripherals such as printers. Also, users can communicate with each other by electronic mail.

Because more than one user might be running programs or accessing files at the same time, networks require software that can support multiple users. Instead of using a single-user operating system, networks must use a network operating system, such as IBM Lan Services or Novell's Netware. Even applications programs must be designed for multiple users.

Users on a network can communicate with each other on-line. They can use electronic mail (*e-mail*) to send and receive messages. They can share the same data files and directories. In some cases, they can communicate in

1

real time, which means that the information entered at one user's keyboard appears on another user's display.

Lessons Learned

- ■ The PC revolution is no more difficult to understand than the home video revolution. PC DOS and your personal computer are about to unlock a new dimension in entertainment and productivity.
- ■ If you feel comfortable with a computer, you can accept and enjoy all that goes with it, just like your VCR.
- ■ Your PC is a product of years of development and more than one company's efforts.
- ■ Computer terminology is simple. The words are basic, and the definitions are easy to understand.
- ■ Hardware, software, screen displays, keyboards, disks, drives, mice, modems, and memory are the tools of microcomputer technology.
- ■ Some PCs are linked into networks, allowing users to share data, software, and peripherals.

In the next chapter, you will learn the different ways to look at DOS.

Looking at DOS

2

The first chapter showed you a bit about how computers evolved, and how peripherals enhance your system. Now it is time to start getting to know DOS.

First impressions are important. For better or worse, we often make snap decisions about people we meet based on their appearance. Once we get to know them, however, we sometimes change our minds.

In this chapter you will get your first good look at DOS. Once you understand what it is you are looking at, you will have no reason to be put-off or intimidated.

2

Key Terms Used in This Chapter	
Current drive	The default disk drive and directory that DOS uses to carry out commands. Unless you change the prompt with a DOS command, the letter of the default drive is the DOS prompt, such as c.
Prompt	A symbol or character(s) that appears on-screen to indicate that you must enter information before anything else can happen.
Directory	A portion of a disk. A directory is like a file folder in a file cabinet. You keep files in directories so that you can isolate a set of files to work with at one time.
Command	An instruction you give to DOS to perform a task.
DOS Shell	A graphical, menu-driven interface that enables you to run DOS commands easily without having to learn the command names.

The Two DOS Views

You have two ways to view DOS and enter commands:

- The DOS Shell view
- The DOS command prompt view

The DOS Shell view is a graphical user interface (GUI). The Shell first appeared in DOS 4 and was greatly improved in DOS 5. In this version of DOS, the Shell remains unchanged in appearance although some functions have been improved. It is described in greater detail later in this chapter and in Chapter 4, "Shell Basics."

The DOS command prompt view is the traditional, simple look of DOS. The command prompt view appears on a plain screen with the DOS prompt. The DOS prompt indicates that DOS is waiting for you to give it a command. If you do not have a hard disk, the standard prompt is one letter of the alphabet that represents the current, or active, drive. The letter is followed by a colon (:), slash (\), and greater-than symbol (>). If you boot, or turn on, your system with the DOS diskette in drive A, the prompt appears as *A:\>* on-screen.

If your computer has a hard disk drive, the standard DOS prompt is the drive letter, followed by a colon (:), followed by the *directory path,* followed by the greater-than symbol (>). After you boot from the hard disk, the prompt appears as *C:\>* on-screen. (The directory path is a complete listing of the drive and the directory. You will learn about directories and the directory path in Chapter 6, "Using Your Hard Disk and Directories.")

Why is the letter B missing? The first diskette drive is always called drive A. The second diskette drive, if present, is always called drive B. The first hard drive, if present, is almost always called drive C. If you have only one diskette drive and a hard drive, the hard drive is called drive C, and DOS treats the diskette drive as both A and B.

The Current Drive

After you turn your PC on, and DOS completes its powering up routine, the command prompt appears, indicating the *current* drive. The current drive is the active drive, or the drive that responds to commands. For example, A:\> tells you that DOS is working from drive A, and B:\> means that DOS is working from drive B.

To switch drives, type the letter of the drive to which you want to switch, followed by a colon, and then press Enter. DOS reads the drive letter and colon as the disk drive's name. For example, if you have a computer with two diskette drives, you can change the current drive from A to B by typing **B:** at the A:\> prompt and pressing Enter.

Before you press Enter, your prompt looks like this:

    A:\>B:

After you press Enter, the following prompt appears:

    B:\>

What does this command mean? It means that you have instructed your PC that you want to work with any information accessible through drive B. It also means that you have begun to take charge!

Many commands automatically use the current drive and other current information. You need not specify the drive if you request information from the current drive. You will learn later how to request information from a drive other than the current drive.

Looking at Directories

When you work with a hard disk, you usually work with one directory at a time. This directory is called the *current directory*. The standard DOS prompt with a hard disk displays the current directory path. If you booted your computer from the hard drive, the current prompt is C:\>. The \ symbol indicates that the root directory is the current directory. The *root* directory is the first directory on your hard disk. It is called the root because it is the directory out of which all other directories grow.

A directory can have subdirectories under it. The complete subdirectory path shows the drive letter and all the directories to the current directory. The complete list of all the directories on a disk is called the *directory tree.*

To make a different directory current, you use the CD (change directory) command. For example, to make DOS the current directory, type **CD DOS** at the C:\> prompt, and then press Enter. The current prompt is now C:\DOS>.

The DOS files are copied to the C:\DOS directory during installation. If you type **DIR /W** at the C:\DOS> prompt and press Enter, DOS displays all the files and any subdirectories in the DOS directory in wide format and then displays the DOS prompt to indicate that it is ready for the next command.

This display shows some of the files in the DOS directory (the top few lines have scrolled up off the screen). The files are displayed by using the DIR /W (directory) command. The current prompt is C:\DOS>.

```
DISPLAY.SYS     DOSHELP.HLP     DOSKEY.COM      DRVLOCK.EXE     E.EXE
E.EX            EDLIN.COM       EGA.CPI         EGA.SYS         EGAX.CPI
EHELP.HLP       EJECT.EXE       EMM386.EXE      EPS.CPI         EXE2BIN.EXE
EXPAND.EXE      FASTOPEN.EXE    FC.EXE          FIND.EXE        GRAPHICS.COM
GRAPHICS.PRO    HELP.EXE        HIMEM.SYS       INTERLNK.EXE    INTERSVR.EXE
ISO.CPI         JOIN.EXE        KEYB.COM        KEYBOARD.SYS    LABEL.COM
LOADFIX.COM     MEM.EXE         MEUTOINI.EXE    MODE.COM        MORE.COM
MOUSE.COM       MOVE.EXE        MSD.EXE         NLSFUNC.EXE     PPDS.CPI
PRINT.COM       RAMDRIVE.SYS    RECOVER.COM     REPLACE.EXE     RESTORE.COM
SETVER.EXE      SHARE.EXE       SMARTDRV.EXE    SORT.EXE        SUBST.EXE
TREE.COM        UNFORMAT.COM    XCOPY.EXE       DOSSWAP.EXE     DRIVER.SYS
POWER.EXE       PRINTER.SYS     UMBCGA.SYS      UMBMONO.SYS     UMBHERC.SYS
UMBEMS.SYS      RAMBOOST.EXE    RAMSETUP.EXE    RAMSETUP.HLP    DATAMON.EXE
VIEW.HLP        DOSSHELL.HLP    DOSSHELL.COM    DOSSHELL.EXE    DOSSHELL.VID
DOSSHELL.INI    GROUP.INI       DOSSHELL.GRB    UNDELETE.EXE    UNDEL.HLP
IBMAVD.EXE      IBMAVD01.HLP    IBMAVD02.HLP    IBMAVD03.HLP    IBMAVD04.HLP
IBMAVD05.HLP    IBMAVD06.HLP    IBMAVD07.HLP    IBMAVD08.HLP    IBMAVD09.HLP
IBMAVD10.HLP    IBMAVD11.HLP    IBMAVDQ.EXE     IBMAVSH.COM     IBMAVSP.EXE
IBMAVDR.BAT     LOCAL.MSG       TUTORIAL.LST    AUTORUN.PRF     ADMIN.PRF
VIRINFO.LST     VIRUS.LST       PRODINFO.LST    VIRSIG.LST      VERV.VDB
CONTACT.LST     DEFAULT.PRF     COMMAND.COM     MEUTOINI.LOG    MOUSE.INI
          130 file(s)     3279649 bytes
                         80709632 bytes free

C:\DOS>
```

A DATA directory is commonly used to contain data files for applications programs. Subdirectories of \DATA contain the files for each application.

```
C:\DATA\TAXES>dir

 Volume in drive C is IBMDOS_6
 Volume Serial Number is 1A83-720A
 Directory of C:\DATA\TAXES

 .            <DIR>      04-03-93    2:54p
 ..           <DIR>      04-03-93    2:54p
 CHECKS   WK1      7819  10-07-91    8:49p
 INCOME   WK1      8483  10-29-92    3:27p
 LOG      DOC     13965  05-17-92   12:50p
 STATEMNT WK1     12031  12-15-91    4:24p
 TAXEST   WK1     21029  01-18-93    3:55p
         7 file(s)      63327 bytes
                     80295936 bytes free

C:\DATA\TAXES>
```

This directory listing displays the data files in the C:\DATA\TAXES directory and is displayed by using the DIR command.

2

The First Look at Commands

You just saw the results of using the CD and DIR commands. DOS 6 has about 100 commands. You will use some of these commands quite often. Many of them you may never use. To issue a command from the DOS command prompt, you type the command and press Enter. COMMAND.COM, the command processor, determines whether you typed the name of a command that is built-in to COMMAND.COM. DIR is an example of a built-in, or *internal,* command. Internal commands are already in the computer's memory; they start as soon as you type the command and press Enter.

When you type a command that is not built-in, COMMAND.COM looks for a program file with the name you typed. These commands are called *external commands.* FORMAT is an example of an external command. You will learn to use FORMAT in Chapter 5.

Most commands require more information than just the command name. For example, to copy a file, you must specify the file or files you want to copy and the destination where you want the files copied. Commands also may have options, called *parameters* or *switches.* The /W you used with the DIR command in a previous example is a parameter. It told DOS to display the directory listing in a wide format. Parameters also tell DOS where and how to run the command. For example, if you type **DIR A:**, you are using a parameter (A:) that specifies that DOS should display a directory list of the files on drive A.

If you correctly type the command at the DOS prompt and then press Enter, the command starts. If you make an error, you receive an error message.

Using the command line, or prompt view, is very fast and easy once you know the commands and their options. When you first start out using DOS, however, the DOS Shell view eliminates the need to know the names of commands and the options.

2

Looking at the DOS Shell

The DOS Shell view is a full-screen graphical window display. You can issue most of the same DOS commands that you type at the DOS prompt by using a mouse or the keyboard to point to and select pull-down menus and dialog boxes. You do not have to remember the names of commands to use the DOS Shell. You just select actions from menus, type answers to questions, and check off options in dialog boxes.

Many shells, desktop publishing programs, and the latest generation of "window style" software were designed for use with a mouse. If, on the other hand, you know your way around a typewriter keyboard, you can perform some functions more quickly in the DOS Shell using cursor keys.

The Shell view is the friendliest way to use DOS commands. For example, a directory listing is automatic when you are in the Shell. You always see a listing of the subdirectories and files in the current directory.

For many users, the Shell is easier to master than DOS, but you still can profit from knowing the DOS commands and terminology. DOS 6 commands remain substantially unchanged from previous versions. The Shell is a shortcut for those who already understand the basics of DOS.

The First Look at the DOS Shell

The DOS Shell has changed very little in DOS 6. The Shell view is a full-screen window with menus and pop-up help screens. The Shell interacts with you in a manner similar to other mouse-and-menu products. For example, if you have ever used Windows, DOS Shell will be familiar to you. If you have never used these types of products, you still will find the Shell very easy to learn and to use. Then, in the future, if you ever use any other mouse-and-menu products, or any Windows applications, you will have a head start.

The Shell provides a visual presentation of DOS, with options from which you make selections. You can manage your computer from the Shell by using graphical alternatives to the DOS prompt commands. You now can also access CP Backup, CP Scheduler, and CP Undelete from the DOS Shell.

Chapter 4, "Shell Basics," discusses the Shell in greater detail. Right now you simply are taking a "first look."

Note: The programs and files listed in your DOS Shell may not match the screen examples shown here. The Directory Tree and files areas specifically reflect the contents of your hard disk. The utilities listed in the program area are the ones you installed with DOS.

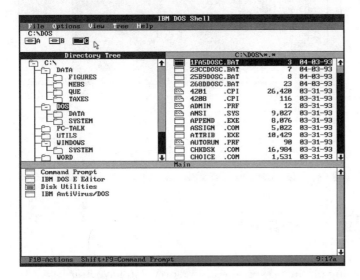

DOS Shell automatically displays information about a disk, a directory, and programs. You use a mouse or the keyboard to move around the display, to select menu items, and to start programs.

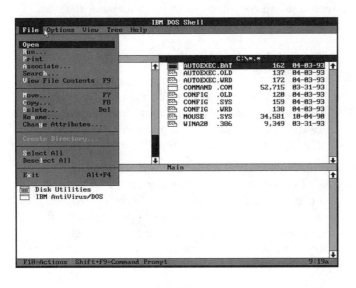

When you make a selection from a menu, the menu commands for that selection pop down.

To move, copy, or rename files or to issue other commands, you don't have to remember command names; you just select items from command menus.

2

When DOS needs you to supply more information to complete a command, DOS displays a dialog box. You type the answers to the prompts, and DOS completes the command.

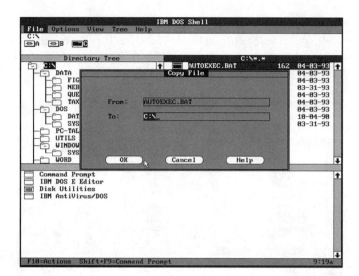

Stopping the Computer

Occasionally you will want to stop the computer from carrying out a command. Besides switching off the power (the last resort), you have four key combinations you can use to stop a command in DOS. Remember that you press and hold the Ctrl key and then press the other key(s) in the sequence.

Ctrl-Break   The Ctrl-Break combination cancels the current process.

Ctrl-C   This key combination stops commands in which DOS pauses for you to type more information. Be aware that DOS carries out many commands too quickly for you to intervene with Ctrl-C.

Ctrl-Alt-Del   This combination is the restart key sequence. Ctrl-Alt-Del should not be your first choice for stopping a command, but sometimes Ctrl-C or Ctrl-Break doesn't work. If the Ctrl-Alt-Del approach fails, turn off the power as a last resort. Some newer computers come with a Reset switch that performs the same function as Ctrl-Alt-Del.

Esc   In DOS and in many applications, pressing the Esc key stops the current process, often reverting to the previous process.

These key sequences are "panic buttons" you can use to stop DOS. Don't worry if you have to use them to prevent disasters. Practice using them with a nondestructive command, such as DIR. You may perspire a little, but soon you will have everything well in hand.

Lessons Learned

- DOS performs commands on the current drive.
- Changing the drive you want to use is as easy as typing a letter and colon.
- When you work with a hard disk, you divide the disk into directories that are like file folders in a file cabinet.
- You can tell DOS to run commands from either the DOS prompt or the Shell.
- The Shell provides an easy way for beginners to run DOS commands. Navigating the Shell is simple, and pull-down menus list all options.
- You can stop the computer from running a command by using one of three Control key combinations.

Now, it is time to learn about DOS files and how they are used.

File Basics

3

Computer files are not unlike the files you keep in your desk drawer. They contain information that is grouped together because of shared characteristics. Instead of being kept in a file cabinet, computer files are stored on the magnetic surface of a disk.

Computer software, including DOS, is made up of files. That means that all of the data stored on your computer system is made up of files. Keeping track of all those files would be difficult if it weren't for DOS.

Once you understand how DOS uses files, you will be able to use DOS to keep all of your computer data organized. In this chapter, you will learn about DOS files and some DOS file conventions.

Disk files are the primary storage place for data and programs. You must know how to manage these files if you want to be in control of your work.

Key Terms Used in This Chapter	
Filename	A description of a file, between one and eight characters long. DOS uses filenames to identify files stored on your computer system.
File extension	Three characters, preceded by a period, added to a filename to further define the type of file.
Wildcard	A character you substitute for another character or characters.

3

Understanding DOS Files

The files on your disks can be divided into a variety of categories. The *filename* can help you determine what type of file it is. A filename can be as long as eight characters or as short as one character. You also can add a period and a three-character *extension* to the filename: SADIE.LET, for example. In many cases, you specify the filename and the program adds the file extension. Over the years, a kind of universal shorthand has evolved to simplify identification of computer files. This identification appears as the extension at the end of the filename, as shown in Table 3.1.

Programs are files that contain computer instructions. Most of the DOS files represent programs. When you buy an *applications program,* you are buying computer instructions to perform certain tasks, such as word processing or spreadsheet manipulation. A program file is called an *executable file* because in computer lingo, to run a program is to execute it. Executable files usually have an EXE file extension.

A *command file* is an executable file in a special format. A command file has a COM file extension. Some of the DOS program files have EXE file extensions and others have COM file extensions. Ignore the different extensions, and treat both types of files as programs.

A *text file* is created by a word processing or text editing program. Text files usually have a TXT or DOC file extension. A text file might be a letter written to your Aunt Sadie in Podunk. Another kind of text file is the one that comes with most software. This file, often titled README.DOC, usually supplies additional instructions for the program that were not included in the printed manual.

Many other types of files and file formats exist. Applications programs might have their own special formats and file extensions. The types of files and file extensions used by DOS are listed in the following tables.

Table 3.1
Examples of the Files That Make Up DOS

Filename	Description
COMMAND.COM, FORMAT.COM, EDLIN.COM	The COM file extension identifies a command file.
EGA.CPI, LCD.CPI	Files with CPI extensions operate the display screen.
AUTOEXEC.BAT	A batch file has the file extension BAT. DOS looks for this batch file and runs it automatically when you start your computer.
BACKUP.EXE, MEM.EXE, CHKDSK.EXE	Executable program files end with EXE.
DOSSHELL.HLP, EHELP.HLP	HLP files display on-screen assistance.
DOSSHELL.INI	INI files are initialization files that contain program default information.
KEYBOARD.SYS, CONFIG.SYS, ANSI.SYS	SYS files are system files. They are also called *device drivers.*

If you ask DOS for a listing of the files contained on a disk, the dot for the extension does not appear. DOS manuals don't explain, but certainly the roots of this curious behavior are sunk deep in the antiquity of DOS folklore. Table 3.2 shows the way filenames appear in an on-screen listing and the way they look when you type them.

Table 3.2
How Filenames Appear

What a file listing looks like on-screen		*What filenames look like when typed*
COMMAND	COM	COMMAND.COM
EGA	CPI	EGA.CPI
AUTOEXEC	BAT	AUTOEXEC.BAT
FIND	EXE	FIND.EXE
DOSSHELL	HLP	DOSSHELL.HLP
DOSSHELL	INI	DOSSHELL.INI
KEYBOARD	SYS	KEYBOARD.SYS

Understanding Filenames and Extensions

A complete filename contains two parts: the name and the extension. A period separates the filename from its extension. In a directory listing, however, spaces separate the filenames and extensions.

In any single directory, each file must have a unique name. DOS treats the filename and the extension as two separate parts. The filenames MYFILE.WK1 and MYFILE.ABC are unique because each file has a different extension. The filenames MYFILE.WK1 and YOURFILE.WK1 are also unique. Many DOS commands make use of the two parts of the filename separately. For this reason, giving each file a name and an extension is a good idea.

Filenames should help you identify the contents of a file. DOS filenames can contain only eight alphanumeric characters, plus a three-character extension. With this built-in limit, meeting the demand of uniqueness and meaningfulness needed for some filenames can require ingenuity.

DOS is also specific about which characters you use in a filename or an extension. To be safe, use only letters of the alphabet and numbers, not spaces or a period. DOS disregards excess characters in a filename.

Considering File Size and Date/Time Stamps

In a standard directory listing, when you type DIR at the prompt, the third column shows the size of the file in bytes. This measurement is an approximation of the size of your file. Your file can actually contain somewhat fewer bytes than shown. Because computers reserve blocks of data storage for files, files with slightly different data amounts may have identical file-size listings. This disk-space allocation method also explains why your word processing memo with only five words can occupy 2K of file space.

3

```
C:\DATA\TAXES>dir

 Volume in drive C is IBMDOS_6
 Volume Serial Number is 1A83-720A
 Directory of C:\DATA\TAXES

.           <DIR>      04-03-93   2:54p
..          <DIR>      04-03-93   2:54p
CHECKS   WK1      7819 10-07-91   8:49p
INCOME   WK1      8403 10-29-92   3:27p
LOG      DOC     13965 05-17-92  12:50p
STATEMNT WK1     12031 12-15-91   4:24p
TAXEST   WK1     21029 01-18-93   3:55p
        7 file(s)     63327 bytes
                   80144384 bytes free

C:\DATA\TAXES>
```

The last two columns in the directory listing display a date and a time.

The time and date stamp represent the time you created the file or, with an established file, the time you last altered the file. Your computer's internal date and time are the basis for the date and time stamp in the directory. As you create more files, the date and time stamps become invaluable tools in determining the most recent version of a file.

Understanding Wildcards

Technically, a *wildcard* is a character in a file specification that depicts one or more characters. You can use wildcards in some commands to tell DOS to execute the command on a series of files. In DOS, the question mark (?) character represents any *single* character. The * represents *all* characters in a filename.

For example, although the command COPY A:*.BAT C: /V looks like hieroglyphics from an Egyptian tomb, all it says is this:

- This is a copy function.
- From the disk in drive A, copy everything (designated by the asterisk) that ends with the three-letter extension BAT.
- Place a copy of these files in drive C.
- And verify (represented by the /V) that the copy is the same as the original.

3

Using Wildcards in the DIR Command

You can use wildcards with the DIR command. The following text provides examples of the use of wildcard characters.

One form of the DIR command looks like this:

```
DIR d:filename.ext
```

When you use DIR alone, DOS lists all files in the current directory. When you use DIR with a filename and extension parameter, DOS lists files that match the parameter. In place of *filename.ext*, you might use the filename MYFILE.WK1, as follows:

```
DIR MYFILE.WK1
```

This DIR command tells DOS to list all files in the current directory matching MYFILE.WK1. The directory lists only one matching file: MYFILE.WK1.

If you want a listing of all files in the current directory that have an extension of WK1, the correct command is

```
DIR *.WK1
```

DOS lists all files (designated by the * character) in the current directory that have the extension WK1. For example, the filenames MYFILE.WK1 and YOURFILE.WK1 both display.

If you issue the command

```
DIR MYFILE.*
```

you might get a listing of MYFILE.WK1 and MYFILE.MEM.

You can use extensions of filenames to specify what the file contains. Files containing correspondence can have the extension LET, and memo files the extension MEM. This practice enables you to use the DIR command with a wildcard to get separate listings of the two types of files.

The ? wildcard differs from the * wildcard. Any character in the precise position as the ? is a match. For example, the command DIR MYFILE?.WK1 lists files such as MYFILE1.WK1 and MYFILE2.WK1, but not MYFILE.WK1. These same rules apply to other commands that allow wildcards.

3

Lessons Learned

■ Files contain information stored on the magnetic surface of a disk.

■ Some files hold instructions; others contain data.

■ Files can be identified by their filenames, and file types can be defined by a three-letter filename extension.

■ A directory listing tells you the filename, the file's size (in bytes), and the time and date of the last update.

■ Wildcards are the shorthand of DOS commands. The asterisk (*) can stand for any number of characters, and the question mark (?) substitutes for one letter in a command.

Now, you are ready to use the DOS Shell to command DOS.

Shell Basics

4

Now that you have the basics of DOS under your belt, you're ready to start taking control. With some earlier versions of DOS, all you had was the manual—a book much more impersonal than this one—and the "dreaded" DOS prompt. If you wanted your computer to do any task, you had to know which words to type and what keys to press; otherwise, nothing happened. If you made a mistake, all you got was an error message. DOS provided no help to guide you. No wonder so many people were afraid of DOS.

That changed with the development of the DOS Shell. Once you enter the DOS Shell, you will find the power of DOS displayed in front of you: no commands to memorize or forget, no filenames to remember, and help at the touch of a key.

The Shell makes DOS much easier to use. You will see the Shell in action in this chapter, and you will be at the controls.

Understanding the DOS Shell display

Selecting with the mouse and keyboard

Using menus, dialog boxes, and scroll bars

Getting help

Running programs from the Shell

Using the Task Swapper

Changing the Shell Display

Finding lost files

Using Undelete

Key Terms Used in This Chapter	
Graphical user interface (GUI)	A graphical way to present information on-screen and to accept information from the user. This type of interface is used in the DOS Shell.
Shell	The interface used to operate DOS.
Icon	A small picture that graphically represents an object such as a file or a program.
Mouse pointer	A symbol, usually an arrow, that shows you the position of the mouse.
Click	The action of pressing the mouse button.
Double-click	The action of quickly pressing the mouse button twice.
Drag	To press and hold down the mouse button as you move the mouse.
Selection cursor	A highlighted band or area that indicates that an item is selected.
Pull-down menu	A secondary menu displayed below the menu bar when you select a menu option.
Dialog box	A window containing options that appears when a command needs additional information.
Shortcut key	A key or key combination you can use in place of a menu selection to issue a command.

Understanding the DOS Shell

When you install and set up DOS 6, you can select to load the DOS Shell automatically. That way, whenever you start your computer the Shell is displayed instead of the command prompt.

If you do not select to have the Shell installed, it will not be loaded. You will not be able to access the DOS Shell unless you re-install DOS.

To start the Shell manually from the DOS prompt:

1. Type **DOSSHELL**.
2. Press Enter.

If you decide you want to exit the DOS Shell and return to the DOS prompt, you have three options:

- Press F3.
- Press Alt-F4.
- Choose **E**xit from the DOS Shell **F**ile menu.

The Shell displays information about your files and programs. You can choose from a number of different ways to display this data. These different views are called *display modes.*

When you start the DOS Shell, you see a full-screen display. This initial display contains much information that is displayed automatically. The display shows you the list of disk drives in your computer, the files in the root directory, and a list of some of the DOS programs available.

If you have an EGA or VGA display, you can display the Shell in *graphics mode.* Changing the display options for this mode is discussed later in this chapter.

In graphics mode, the Shell uses *icons*—small pictures—to represent disk drives, directories, programs, and text files. Other parts of the shell, such as the scroll bars and the mouse pointer, are easier to read in graphics mode.

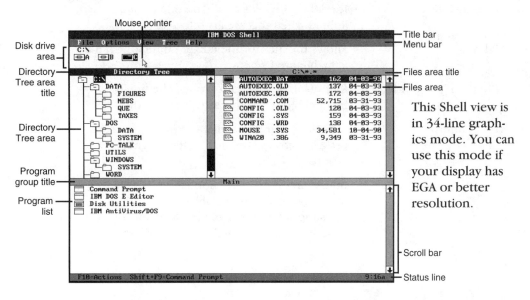

This Shell view is in 34-line graphics mode. You can use this mode if your display has EGA or better resolution.

4

4

See Table 4.1 for a description of the basic parts of the Shell display.

Table 4.1
DOS Shell Parts

Part	Description
Title bar	Identifies the name of the current window or dialog box.
Menu bar	Provides a list of pull-down menu options. The menu bar is below the title bar of the main window.
Disk drive area	Lists the disk drives that your computer recognizes. The selected drive is highlighted. Drives A and B are diskette drives. The first hard disk drive is C. If your hard disk drive or drives are partitioned into separate logical drives, each drive letter is treated as a separate physical drive.
Directory Tree area title	Identifies the Directory Tree area. The title is highlighted when this area is selected.
Directory Tree area	Shows the directories for the selected drive. The current directory is highlighted.
Files area title	Identifies the Files area. The title is highlighted when this area is selected.
Files area	Shows the files for the current directory. A file is highlighted.
Program group title	Identifies the program group. The title is highlighted when this area is selected.
Program list	Lists the programs available from the current program group, and lists other program groups.
Selection cursor	In text mode, the selection cursor is a small triangular arrow. In graphics mode, it indicates the selected drive, directory, file, or program with a highlighted area or band.

Part	Description
Status line	Shows function key commands, messages, and the current time at the bottom line of the Shell area.
Mouse pointer	Indicates the current position of the mouse on the display. You use the mouse pointer to select items.
Scroll bars	Scrolls any list of directories, files, or programs that is too long to fit in the display area.

From the Shell you can issue DOS commands, run programs, find files, view the contents of files, and change the way that the Shell area appears. All these actions are performed by selecting menu options. You do not have to remember command names or the format and parameters of the commands. Just browse through the Shell to see the available commands.

If you decide you want to use the command line, you can select Exit from the File menu, press Alt-F4, use the Exit shortcut keys, or press the F3 function key.

Selecting Items

The concept of selecting an *item* and then performing some action with that item is one of the main concepts behind the Shell graphical user interface. An item can be a disk, a directory, a file, or a program. You select an item by using either the mouse or the keyboard. You select an action from a menu or by using a *shortcut key,* as explained in the section "Making Menu Selections" later in this chapter.

Using the Mouse

Although you can use the Shell with the keyboard or the mouse, you will find that using the mouse is much easier. The graphical user interface was designed to be used with a mouse. In fact, the mouse was designed and developed specifically to control a graphical interface.

With the mouse, you can select items and menu options. As you move the mouse, the mouse pointer moves in the same direction on-screen. The mouse pointer takes on different shapes in the various modes of DOS 6. In graphics mode, for example, the mouse pointer is an arrow. In text mode, the mouse pointer is a colored rectangle. In addition, the mouse pointer sometimes changes shape to indicate the action taking place.

To select an item with the mouse, make sure that the tip of the mouse pointer is over the item you want to select and *click* the left mouse button. Your mouse may have two or three buttons, but unless otherwise indicated you should use the left button.

When you click a mouse button, you press and release the button once without moving the mouse. Don't press too hard. Gentle pressure with one finger is all that is needed to click the mouse. If you press too hard, you may move the mouse as you click, thereby making the wrong selection.

You should be familiar with mouse terminology. To *click* an item means to move the mouse pointer until it is over the item and then click the mouse. At times, you *double-click* the mouse, which means to click the mouse twice in rapid succession. To *drag* an object with the mouse, move the mouse pointer over an object and then press and hold down the mouse button as you move the object with the mouse pointer. Unlike the keyboard cursor keys, you can move the mouse in any direction: up, down, left, right, or at any angle.

Move the mouse pointer to the folder icon next to C:\ in the Directory Tree area. Click the left mouse button; the directory tree alternately expands (to show all branches) and collapses (to show no branches).

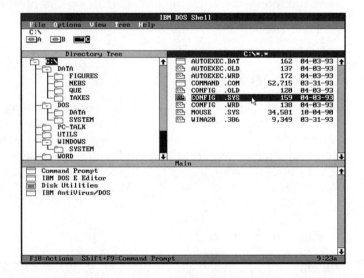

Try moving the mouse pointer to the icon next to *Disk Utilities* in the program list. Double-click the left mouse button and the program group title switches from *Main* to *Disk Utilities*. The program list now displays the DOS disk utilities. Double-click the icon next to *Main* to switch back to the *Main* program list.

Using the Keyboard

Although slower than using a mouse, the keyboard works just as well. To use the keyboard to select an item, use any of the following procedures:

- Press the Tab key to select the area you want. Pressing Tab highlights the selected area title. If no title bar is highlighted, the selected area is the disk drive area near the top of the display.

- Press Shift-Tab to move back to the previously selected area.

- After you are in the appropriate area, use the up- and down-arrow keys to move the selection cursor to the directory, file, or program you want to select.

- In the disk drives area, use the left- and right-arrow keys to select a different disk drive.

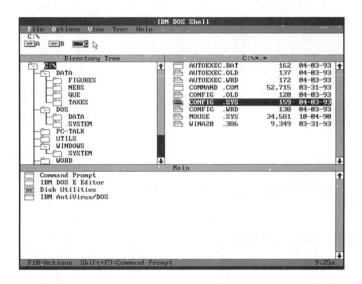

If no title bar is highlighted, the selection cursor is in the disk drives area.

Making Menu Selections

Performing tasks in the Shell is similar to performing tasks in real life. When you want to open a file in the Shell, you first select the File menu (the object), and then you select **O**pen (the action). This process can be compared to selecting a pair of shoes (the object), and then putting them on (the action).

Most often you choose an action from a menu. The initial menu options are listed in the menu bar. The possible menu selections are **File**, **Options**, **View**, **Tree**, and **Help**. When the program list is highlighted, the **Tree** menu is not available.

When you select a menu option, a *pull-down menu* is displayed. From the pull-down menu, you select the specific action you want to use, such as a DOS command. Menu options that appear dimmer than others are unavailable for selection. Sometimes, depending on the color scheme you select, they do not appear at all.

Some menu options remain dim if you do not have a file or text selected. Most of the options in the File menu, for example, require something to be highlighted before the option is available for use; options in many of the other menus do not require anything to be selected.

4

When you choose a menu option, DOS displays a pull-down menu with a list of commands.

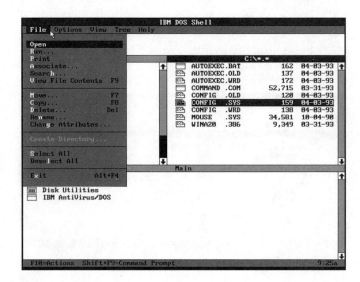

Using the Mouse with Menus

Selecting a menu option and a command from the pull-down menu with a mouse is easy. Follow these steps:

1. Move the mouse pointer to the menu option and click the mouse button.
2. Move the mouse pointer to the menu command you want to use and click the mouse button again.

Using the Keyboard with Menus

To select a menu option and a command from the pull-down menu with the keyboard, follow these steps:

1. Press [Alt] or [F10] to access the menu bar.

   This action highlights the File menu bar item.

2. Press [←] or [→] to highlight the menu bar option you want.

3. Press [↓] to access the pull-down menu.

4. Press [↓] or [↑] to highlight the menu item you want.

5. Press [↵Enter] to select the menu item.

You also can use another keyboard method to make selections from a menu more quickly. This second method is faster, but may feel awkward at first if you are a beginner.

For the quick keyboard method, follow these steps:

1. Press [Alt] or [F10] to access the menu bar.

   This action highlights the File menu bar item.

2. Type the underlined or highlighted letter of the menu bar item you want.

   This step opens the pull-down menu for that menu bar item.

3. Type the underlined or highlighted letter of the menu item you want to use.

Using Shortcut Keys

A *shortcut key* enables you to press a key or combination of keys instead of selecting a menu item. Some of the most common menu items have shortcut keys. Although you don't have to use shortcut keys, these keys do save time when you use a menu item often.

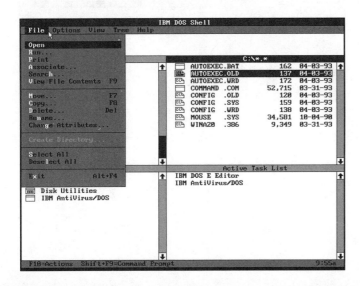

Shortcut keys are listed next to the menu item in the pull-down menus. If no key is listed, that command has no shortcut key. If two keys are listed together, press both keys at the same time.

Cancelling Menus

If you select a menu in error, you can cancel the selection and make a different menu selection. To cancel a menu with the mouse, just click anywhere
outside the menu area, or click the right mouse button. To cancel a menu
with the keyboard, press Esc.

If you make the wrong menu selection with the mouse, just click on the
correct menu option in the menu bar. The incorrect pull-down menu disappears, and the new menu opens. If you make the wrong menu selection with
the keyboard, just press the left-arrow or right-arrow key to select the menu
choice you want.

4

Using Dialog Boxes

Sometimes you must enter additional information before DOS can carry out
the command you selected. When DOS needs additional information, it opens
a dialog box. When a command has a dialog box, the command name in the
pull-down menu is followed by an ellipsis (...). A dialog box may request one
piece of information or many separate pieces of information, depending on
the command.

If you choose File
Display Options
from the Options
menu, for ex-
ample, DOS
opens a dialog
box that enables
you to change the
way data is
displayed in the
files area.

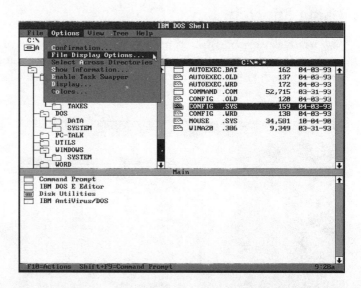

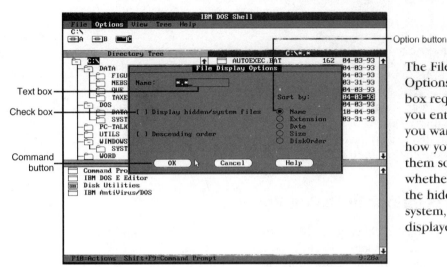

Text box

Check box

Command button

Option button

The File Display Options dialog box requests that you enter the files you want to see, how you want them sorted, and whether you want the hidden, or system, files displayed.

The dialog box is one of the most powerful features of a graphical user interface. With some menu systems, you must choose many different levels of menus to get to the one you want. Often, you must make more than ten selections to start one command. With pull-down menus and dialog boxes, however, you select a menu and a command; then, if additional information is needed, DOS prompts you for that information in a dialog box, which can be as large as a full screen if necessary.

Dialog boxes can contain the following elements:

- A *text box*—a box in which you type text, such as a filename.

- A *check box*—an on-and-off or yes-or-no question enclosed in square brackets. If the option is selected, an X appears in the square brackets.

- An *option button*—a circle next to a specific option. The selected option has a black dot in the circle. Related option buttons are grouped together. You can choose only one option button at a time from a group.

- A *list box*—similar to a list of option buttons, but in a different format. You can choose only one option from the list.

- A *command button*—represents a possible action you can take from the dialog box. The OK button processes the command. The Cancel button cancels the command. The Help button displays on-line help for the dialog box.

Entering Text in Dialog Boxes

To use the mouse to select a text box in a dialog box, move the mouse pointer to the text box and click the left mouse button. If you are using the keyboard, press Tab or Shift-Tab to move to the text box.

To type over an existing entry, just type the new entry. To change an existing entry, press the left-arrow or right-arrow key to position the cursor. Press Backspace to delete a character to the left of the cursor and Del to delete the character at the cursor; then type any new text.

Selecting Options in Dialog Boxes

To select or deselect a check box with a mouse, move the mouse pointer between the square brackets and click. To use the keyboard, press Tab or Shift-Tab to move to the check box, and then press the space bar.

To use the mouse to select an option from a list of option buttons, move the mouse pointer to the option button and click. A black dot appears in the selected option button and disappears from any other button in the list. If you click the black dot, nothing happens. With a keyboard, use the up-arrow and down-arrow keys to move the black dot to the option you want to select. Although you can select multiple items from a list of check boxes, you can select only one option from a list of option buttons.

In some dialog boxes, a list of possible options is displayed in a box. You select from this list. To select an option from a list box with the mouse, move the mouse pointer to the option you want and click. With the keyboard, use the down-arrow and up-arrow keys to highlight the option you want.

This list box enables you to select from a number of different color schemes, depending on the type of display you have.

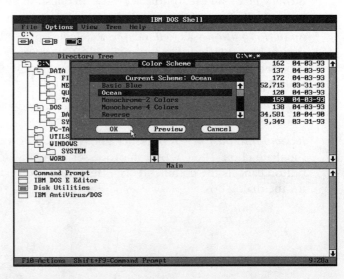

Using Command Buttons

After you supply the requested information in a dialog box, you select the OK command button to start the command with your choices. Select the Cancel button to ignore all information entered in the dialog box and cancel the command. Other command buttons might be available, such as Help.

To select a command button with the mouse, move the mouse pointer to the button and click the left mouse button. If you are using the keyboard, press Tab or Shift-Tab until an underline appears on the command button you want; then press Enter or the space bar. You can press Esc to cancel a command at any time.

4

Using Scroll Bars

Sometimes a list is too long to fit within a display area or dialog box. If you use a mouse, you can use *scroll bars* to view text that is not visible. The scroll bar runs the length of a list. The *scroll box* is a gray, rectangular box inside the scroll bar. The scroll box represents the position and the fraction of the data in the currently displayed list. In this Directory Tree area, the scroll box starts at the top of the scroll bar, which means that the top of the list of directories is displayed.

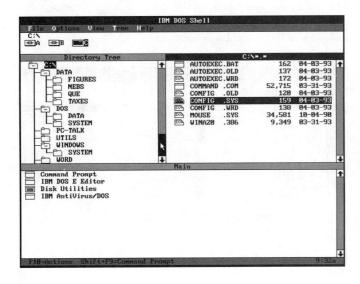

To scroll down a list, click the black area of the scroll bar, below the scroll box. The scroll box moves down and the list scrolls down to display another part of the list.

4

After you click below the scroll box, the text scrolls down. You can keep clicking until the scroll box reaches the bottom, revealing the bottom of the list of directories.

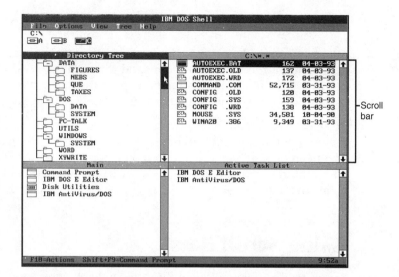

At the top and bottom of the scroll bar is a *scroll arrow*—an arrow you can click to scroll the screen in the direction of the arrow. To scroll up or down by one line, move the mouse pointer to the up scroll arrow or the down scroll arrow and click. For every click, the display scrolls one line and the scroll box moves accordingly.

The size of the scroll box tells you how much of the list is visible. If the scroll box is small compared to the total length of the scroll bar, the list is long and you can see only a small part of the list at any one time.

The DOS directory contains about 130 files. The scroll box indicates that only a small fraction of the files in the list are visible.

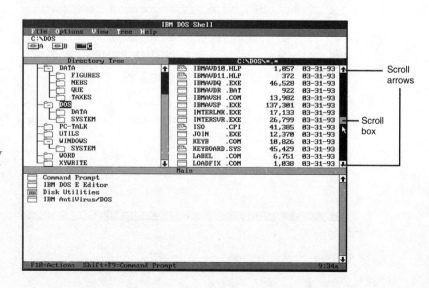

When a list is long, you can scroll swiftly by dragging the scroll box. To drag a scroll box, move the mouse pointer to the scroll box, hold down the right mouse button, and move the pointer up or down. As long as you keep the mouse button pressed while you move the mouse, the scroll box moves with the mouse pointer and also scrolls the list.

To scroll with the keyboard, press Tab to select the area you want; then press the up-arrow or down-arrow key to move the selection cursor one item at a time in the direction of the arrow. Press PgUp or PgDn to scroll up or down, respectively, one full screen at a time.

Getting On-Line Help

4

DOS Shell has on-line help available to you at all times. To get help for a specific menu item, command, or dialog box, select the item for which you want help and press F1. For general help with using the Shell, commands, procedures, or the keyboard, select the Help item from the menu bar.

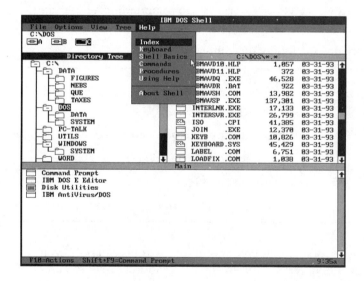

General on-line help is always available with the Help menu bar item. Select any of the Help menu items for additional help information.

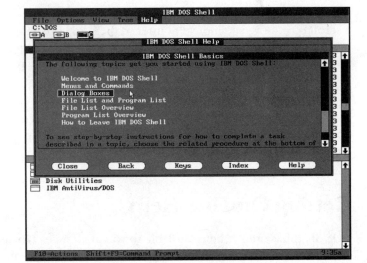

Shell Basics help topics are high-lighted on the Help screen.

4

To use the mouse to get help on any of the general help topics, double-click on a topic. If you are using the keyboard, press Tab to underline a topic, and then press Enter.

Each Help screen contains the following command buttons:

Command Button	Description
Close	Cancels help
Back	Displays previous Help screen
Keys	Displays help on keyboard keys
Index	Displays the Help index
Help	Displays help on how to use the Help system

You will notice that in most help screens, several terms appear in bold type. By double-clicking on a bold term, you can "jump" to another help screen on that particular topic. Use the Back button when you are ready to return to the Help screen from which you jumped.

Running Programs from the Shell

This section introduces the idea of starting programs from the Shell. Programs are files that have an EXE or COM file extension. Batch files with a BAT file extension contain DOS commands and start programs.

You can start a program or batch file in several ways. You can select **Run** from the File menu, type the name of the program, and press Enter. Alternatively, you can select the program or batch file in the files area and press Enter.

Perhaps the most convenient way to start a program is by selecting it from the list of programs that appears in the lower portion of your screen. You can add your favorite programs to this area. Notice that when you are in the program list, the File menu has different options than when you are in the disk drive, Directory Tree, or file areas. From this modified File menu, select the **New** command to add your favorite program to the program list.

After the program completes its processing or you exit from the program, you see the message `Press any key to return to DOS Shell`. After you press a key, you return to the Shell.

Using the Task Swapper

A powerful feature of the DOS Shell is the *Task Swapper*. With the Swapper enabled, you can run more than one program at the same time and switch between them. This feature can be handy if you regularly use more than one program, such as a word processor and a spreadsheet, and often change between them.

To enable the Task Swapper, select the Options menu, and then select **Enable Task Swapper**. A black diamond appears to the left of the command on the menu to indicate that the Swapper is enabled.

When the Task Swapper is enabled, the program area at the bottom of the screen is split into two areas. The Active Task List area lists all programs that have been started.

With the Swapper enabled, you can start a program, and then suspend the program and return to the Shell. To return to the Shell from a program, press Alt-Esc. Once back in the Shell, you can start one or more other programs, which also can be suspended by pressing Alt-Esc.

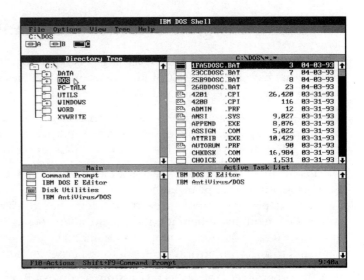

In this example, the IBM DOS E Editor and the IBM AntiVirus/DOS programs are running as active tasks, and current action has been returned to the Shell.

4

When you start one or more programs and return to the Shell, the programs are listed in the Active Task List area. To resume an active task, double-click the task name, or select the task and press Enter.

When you return to an active task, you return to the exact environment you left. The same file or files are in memory, the cursor is in the same spot, and any options are unchanged. The Task Swapper is so handy, you may want to leave it enabled.

It is important to remember to quit all active tasks before you leave the DOS Shell or shut off your computer. If you do not, you run the risk of damaging your program files.

Changing the Shell Display

As you can see, a great deal of information is available to you in the DOS Shell area. You are in control of this area. You can change the way the Shell looks in a number of ways.

Changing the Shell View

The Shell view used so far has three or four areas: a directory area, a files area, a program area, and if the Swapper is enabled, an active task list area. You can change this display with the View menu options. Each display choice is called a *view*. Five possible view choices are available.

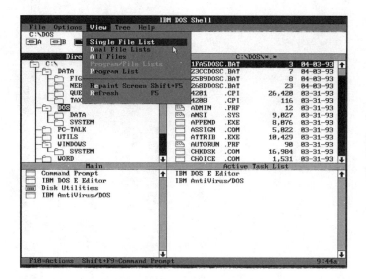

The View menu shows the possible view choices.

The default view is Program/File Lists. This view lists directories and files at the top of the screen and programs at the bottom of the screen. The current view choice appears gray or dim on the View menu because you cannot change the view to the current view. Program/File Lists is the most common view because it permits you to work with both files and programs at the same time.

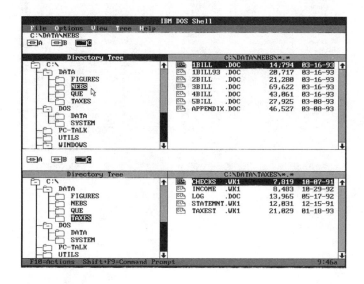

The Dual File Lists view is handy when you want to copy or move files. You can display two directories on the same disk or on different disks at the same time.

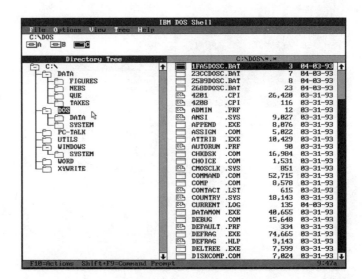

The Single File
List view is handy
when you want to
look at a large
group of files.
With this view,
you can see the
entire directory
tree and many
more files in the
DOS directory.

4

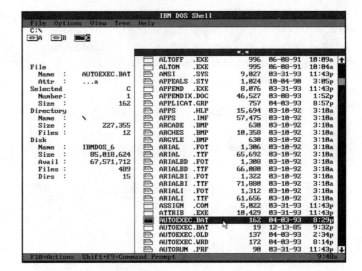

The All Files view
lists every file
on the disk, in
alphabetical
order, regardless
of the directory.

The All Files view is handy when you are trying to locate a specific file or looking for duplicate filenames in different directories.

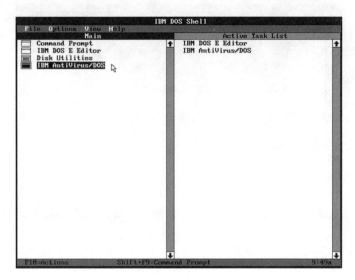

The Program List view is useful if you are using a long list of programs and they do not all fit in the program area with the Program/File Lists view. The Program List view is also a useful tool in setting up your system; you don't have to directly access directories.

Changing the Shell Display Mode

The way information appears on-screen is controlled by the display/screen mode. In figures at the beginning of this chapter, you saw the Shell in 25-line text mode and then in 34-line graphics mode. You have a number of display mode options. The best display mode for your system depends on the type of display adapter you have and the size of your display. You can try different options and select the one you like best.

The options described here are available if you have a VGA display. If you have a different display adapter, you may see different options.

To change the display mode, choose Display from the Options menu. DOS displays the Screen Display Mode dialog box.

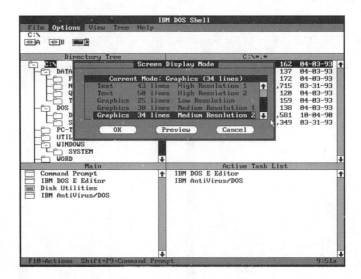

Scroll through the screen modes available for your computer system. Choose the Preview button to see what a screen mode looks like on your display. When you find the screen mode you like, choose OK.

Changing the Shell Colors

If you have a color display, you can view the Shell in color. You have a choice of available color schemes. Ocean is the color scheme selected for the screens used to illustrate this book; the screens are printed, of course, in shades of gray.

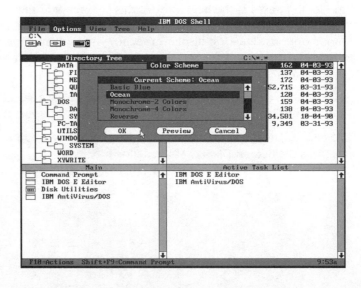

To change the color scheme, select Colors from the Options menu. The Color Scheme dialog box opens.

Scroll through the color schemes available for your computer system. You can choose the Preview button to see what a color scheme looks like on your display. When you find the color scheme you like, choose OK.

Finding Lost Files

Now you have control of the Shell, and you have seen how it simplifies using commands. The DOS Shell also lets you work with the files on your disk. It can make file organization a breeze. For example, it can help you keep track of all the files you have stored, including finding lost files and recovering files that have been deleted.

The DOS Shell gives you many ways to find lost files. You can use the Search option from the File menu; you can change the Shell view and the file display options; or, if a file has been deleted, you may be able to recover it using the PC DOS Undelete utility. You will learn how to change the file display options in Chapter 6, "Using Your Hard Disk and Directories."

Using Search

If you know the name or extension of the file you need to find, or even if you only know part of the name or extension, you can use Search to find it. You can use wildcard characters if you want to search for a series of files. To search for one or more files, follow these steps:

1. Press Alt-F or click on File to activate the File menu.

2. Choose Search from the File menu. The Search File dialog box opens.

3. In the Search for text box, enter the name of the file you want to find. You may use wildcards. To search for all the files with a .WK1 extension, for example, type *.**WK1** in the text box.

4. To search the entire disk, select the Search entire disk check box. To search only the current directory, deselect the Search entire disk check box.

5. Select OK.

6. DOS lists all the files it finds on the Search Results screen.

7. Press Esc to return to the main DOS Shell screen from the Search Results screen.

Enter *.**WK1** in the Search File dialog box to tell DOS to find all the files with a .WK1 extension.

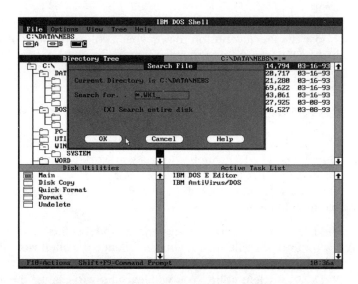

DOS displays the Search Results screen listing all the files on the disk with a .WK1 extension.

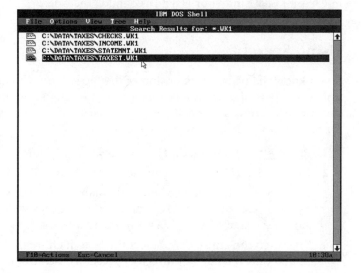

Using Central Point Undelete

If you delete a file or group of files in error, you might be able to recover them using the Central Point Undelete utility. CP Undelete offers three levels of file protection—Delete Sentry, Delete Tracker, and DOS. Delete Sentry and Delete Tracker are memory-resident programs that must be loaded at the command line. The basic DOS level of protection, however, is active whenever you start your computer.

If you use the Undelete utility immediately after you delete a file, DOS ensures that you will be able to recover it. If you do not use Undelete immediately, it is possible that DOS will place a new file on the part of the disk that stored the deleted file. In that case, you may not be able to recover the deleted file.

To use CP Undelete, follow these steps:

1. Select Central Point Undelete from the program area. Using the keyboard, highlight it and press Enter. Using the mouse, double-click it. The CP Undelete screen opens.

    The CP Undelete screen looks similar to the DOS Shell screen. The top portion of the screen contains a disk drive area, on the left is the Directory Tree, on the right is the file area, and a status line occupies the bottom of the screen.

2. Select the files from the list of deleted files that you want to undelete. You can select one or several files. Using the keyboard, highlight the file you want to undelete and press Enter. If you are using the mouse, click on the filename you want to undelete. Repeat this for each file you want to recover. Selected files will appear highlighted or in a different color.

4

Notice that the files in the file area are all missing a first letter, such as in the entry *?CREEN00.PCX*. This missing letter indicates that these files have been deleted.

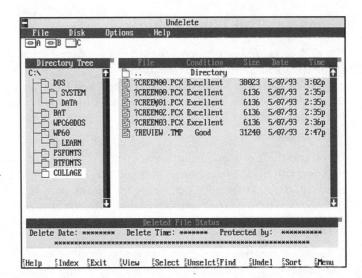

3. To undelete the selected files choose File Undelete; a dialog box appears and asks for a new first letter for the name of the file you want to recover. After you type the letter, press Enter twice.

The Enter First Character dialog box asks you to enter a new first letter for the deleted file. The original filename was destroyed when the file was deleted.

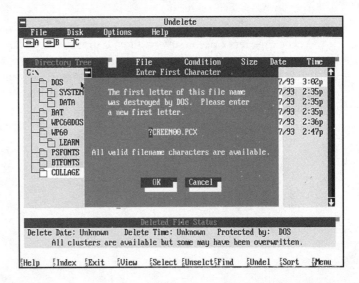

4. After the file is recovered, you are returned to the CP Undelete screen. Notice that the file you selected to undelete, *?CREEN00.PCX* in this case, has been replaced by the recovered file, *SCREEN00.PCX*.

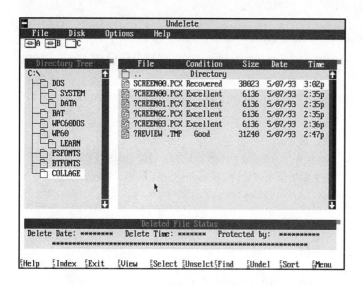

The condition of the file changes from Excellent to Recovered.

5. Press F3 or Alt-F4 to leave CP Undelete and return to the DOS Shell. When you return to the Shell, the undeleted files are not included in the file list display. Make sure the program area is not active and press F5 to refresh the display. The undeleted files will appear.

Central Point Undelete also has a feature that enables you to search by name for specific files that have been deleted. You can access the Find Deleted Files dialog box from the CP Undelete File menu.

Leaving the DOS Shell

Although you will find that you can do almost all computer work from the Shell, you will sometimes want to work from the command prompt. You can exit the Shell in two ways. You can quit the Shell and remove it from memory, or you can suspend it temporarily.

If the Task Swapper is enabled, you must first exit all active tasks before you can quit the Shell. To quit the Shell, you can do any of the following:

- Press F3.
- Press Alt-4.
- Choose Exit from the File menu.

To return to the Shell from the command line, type **DOSSHELL** at the prompt and press Enter.

To suspend the Shell temporarily to use the DOS prompt, you can do one of the following:

- Press Shift-9.
- Select Command Prompt from the program area and press Enter.

To resume the Shell, type **EXIT** at the DOS prompt and press Enter. You return to the Shell, and any active tasks remain active.

Lessons Learned

- The DOS Shell is an easy-to-use graphical interface.
- A mouse is the fastest and easiest way to use the Shell, but using the keyboard is also easy.
- You can use the Shell to perform many DOS commands and run programs without knowing the names of commands.
- To use the Shell, you first select an item and then select an action. An item can be a disk, a directory, a file, or a program.
- You select items from lists and actions from menus. You don't have to memorize names of items or actions.
- On-line help is always just a keystroke away.
- You can use the Shell to find files and to undelete files.

In the next chapter, you will learn how to prepare and protect your disks and diskettes.

Using Disks and Diskette Drives

5

Do you remember the feeling of starting school with a desk full of new notebooks? The pages covered with empty lines practically begged to be filled with information. Tabs were labeled and subjects were identified. Even if this organization was short-lived, at least for now you were ready.

Preparing your computer to hold and organize information can be an even more pleasing experience. Learning to format disks is easy if you are willing to take your time. DOS does the hard part, and you don't even have to worry about poor penmanship.

When you work with diskettes, keep the following ideas in mind:

- Always keep the labels on your diskettes current. Use a felt-tipped pen to write the contents on the diskette label as you work. Diskettes not labeled, or labeled incorrectly, are an invitation to lost data. If you do not label diskettes, you might mistake them for blank, unformatted diskettes.

- Never use a ball point pen to write on a label that has been placed on a $5\frac{1}{4}$-inch diskette. The jacket doesn't keep the pen point from possibly damaging the magnetic media and harming the diskette.

Key Terms Used in This Chapter	
Format	Initial preparation of a disk for data storage.
Volume label	A disk-level name that identifies a particular disk.
Track	A circular section of a disk's surface that holds data.
Sector	A section of a track that acts as the disk's smallest storage unit.
Allocation unit	A group of sectors that DOS uses to keep track of files on the disk.
Reformat	To format a diskette that has already been formatted but that stores information you no longer need.
Unformat	To recover the files on a disk after it has been formatted.
Duplicate	To make an exact copy of a diskette.
Software virus	A set of instructions hidden inside a computer program, designed to wreak havoc on your computer system.

Understanding Diskettes

A diskette is a Mylar pancake in a plastic dust cover. The Mylar diskette is covered with magnetic material similar to the metallic coating on recording tape. Out of the box, diskettes usually aren't ready for you to use. You must *format* them first. Some diskettes are *preformatted,* meaning that they are ready for use.

DOS's FORMAT command performs the preparation process for disks. You simply enter the command, and FORMAT analyzes for disk defects, generates a root directory, sets up a storage table (called a *file allocation table*), and alters other parts of the diskette.

The magnetic disk is like unlined paper—hardly a good medium for proper magnetic penmanship. If you use blank pages, you could wind up with wandering, uneven script. Lines on the paper serve as guides to help keep you on track. Although you can write on unlined paper, DOS is not that flexible. Your computer cannot use a disk at all until it is formatted.

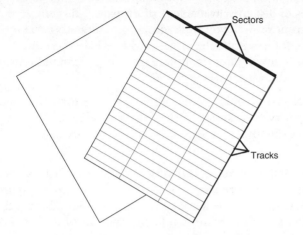

Formatted disks can be compared to lined paper, with horizontal lines subdivided by vertical lines.

5

Just as lines on paper are guides for the writer, tracks and sectors on a disk are guides for the computer. Because the storage medium of a spinning disk is circular, the "premarked lines," or magnetic divisions called *tracks,* are placed in concentric circles. These tracks are further subdivided into areas called *sectors.*

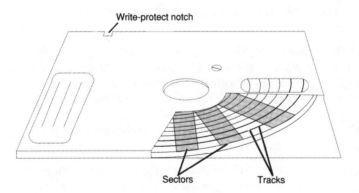

When you format a blank disk, DOS magnetically encodes (marks) tracks and sectors onto the disk's surface.

DOS decides what type of drive you have and then positions the tracks and sectors accordingly. DOS stores data in these sectors and uses both the track and sector numbers to find and retrieve information.

Understanding Diskette Formats

Before you can buy the right diskettes for your computer, you must understand the different types of diskettes available. Unfortunately, diskettes are described in many different ways. If you walk into a computer store to buy 1.44 megabyte diskettes, for example, the boxes might reveal everything except the capacity. The following information helps you understand how to buy the different types of diskettes you may need.

Diskettes differ in capacity, size, and number of tracks and sectors. Over the years, the maximum capacity of diskettes has increased steadily. In 1981, a diskette could hold 160K (kilobytes). Today, 2.88M diskettes are starting to appear.

The easy part of understanding diskettes is determining the size. Two sizes are available: 5 ¼-inch and 3 ½-inch. The larger disks were available first and are more common. The smaller disks have a higher capacity, have rigid cases that protect the disk from damage, and are more reliable. The size of the disks is clearly marked on the box and is easy to determine from the size of the box itself.

Diskettes can be either *single-sided* or *double-sided*. Double-sided diskettes have tracks on both sides of the disk and, therefore, twice the capacity of single-sided diskettes. Only double-sided diskettes are used in today's PCs. Some computer stores may still sell single-sided diskettes for very old PCs and other computers. Boxes of diskettes should be labeled *two-sided, 2S, double-sided,* or *DS*.

Diskettes come in different *densities.* The density is a measure of how closely the bytes of information are placed on the disk. Today, diskettes are either double-density or high-density. High-density is sometimes called *quad-density*. Single-density diskettes have never been used in PCs, but they have been used in older types of computers. Double-density diskettes usually are labeled *DD* or *2DD* (the *2* means double-sided), and high-density diskettes are labeled *HD* or *2HD*.

Sectors on all types of diskettes hold 512 bytes (.5K). Diskettes have different capacities because they have more sectors per track or more tracks per side.

The standard diskettes generally used are summarized in the following list:

Disk Type	Sectors per Track	Tracks per Side	Capacity
5 ¼-inch			
Double-density	9	40	360K
High-density	15	80	1.2M
3 ½-inch			
Double-density	9	80	720K
High-density	18	80	1.44M
	36	80	2.88M

720K diskettes are often labeled *1M,* and 1.44M disks are often labeled *2M.* These numbers refer to the unformatted capacity of the disk and, unfortunately, add to the confusion.

You don't need to remember all this information about diskettes because the computer and DOS handle this information for you. When you buy disks and when you format them, however, you should understand that different types of disks are available.

Matching Diskettes and the Diskette Drive

Just as there are different types of diskettes, there are different types of diskette drives. The most obvious difference is the diskette drive size. Drives can be either 5 ¼-inch or 3 ½-inch. If you have one or two 5 ¼-inch drives, you cannot use 3 ½-inch diskettes, and vice versa. If you have one drive of each size, you can read both sizes of disks.

Size is not the only consideration, however. Disk drives also have a maximum capacity. A 5 ¼-inch drive might be a standard (360K) drive or a high-capacity (1.2M) drive. A 1.2M drive can read and write 360K disks, but a 360K drive cannot read or write 1.2M disks. The 1.2M diskettes fit in the drive, but you cannot use them.

Although you can use 360K diskettes in 1.2M drives, the results can be unreliable at times. If you write to a 360K disk in a 1.2M drive, you should have no trouble reading that disk in the same drive. You may, however, have trouble

5

reading the disk in a 360K drive. This problem is intermittent and occurs more often with older drives. Keep this in mind if you copy files onto a diskette to be read by another computer. If you run into this problem, try using another diskette or reformat the diskette.

The same situation exists with 3 ½-inch drives. If you have a 720K drive, you cannot use 1.44M diskettes. If you have 1.44M drives, you can use both types of 3 ½-inch diskettes.

Formatting Diskettes

As formatting your diskettes becomes a routine task, remember to use care. Formatting clears all information that a diskette contains. If you format a diskette you have used earlier, everything stored on that diskette disappears. Be careful not to format diskettes that contain files you want to keep. Labeling your diskettes helps you avoid such a mishap. You also should use the DIR command to check the list of files on a diskette before you try to format a used diskette.

Place some type of indicator on each diskette you format to avoid mistaking formatted diskettes for unformatted diskettes. The indicator may be as simple as a dot, a check mark, or the letter *F* for *formatted.* When you buy diskettes, adhesive labels are included. A simple method to keep track of formatted diskettes is to put a label on each diskette that you format. Then you know that a diskette without a label has never been formatted.

To format a diskette from the Shell, you must access the Format utility, which is located in the Disk Utilities program group. When you first start the Shell, the program area at the bottom is labeled *Main.* This label refers to the Main *program group* that DOS sets up when you install DOS on your hard disk. Program groups are like file folders that contain related programs.

DOS sets up the Main and Disk Utilities program groups automatically. To format a disk from the Shell, you must access the Format program, located in the Disk Utilities program group.

5

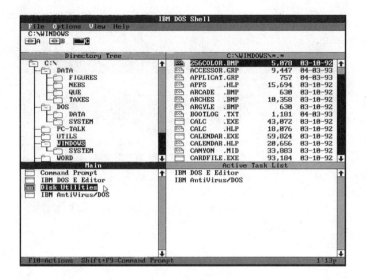

You can tell that Disk Utilities is a program group and not a program because its icon is different.

To start a program from the Shell, first you open the program group, and then you select the program in that group.

To use the Shell to format a diskette, follow these steps:

1. Open the Disk Utilities group by double-clicking on it, or select it and press ↵Enter.

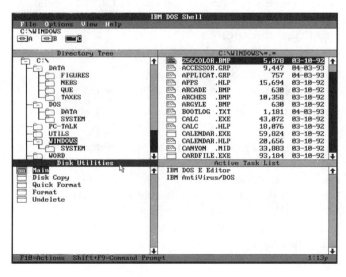

The Disk Utilities program group contains DOS commands that help you manage disks. In Chapter 4, "Shell Basics," you learned to use Undelete from the Disk Utilities program group.

2. Issue the Format command by double-clicking Format or by selecting Format and pressing ↵Enter.

The Format
dialog box opens.

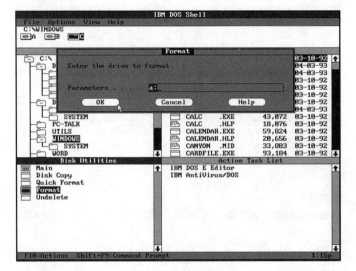

If you have two diskette drives, you can format diskettes in either drive A or B. When you use the Shell to format a diskette, DOS assumes that you want to use drive A. If you want to format the diskette with no special options, you can accept the default and choose OK. To format a diskette in drive B, type b:. When you type anything in the text box, the highlighted default text disappears.

3. Choose OK from the Format dialog box.

Even if you have already put a diskette in the drive before you started the format, DOS prompts you to insert a diskette into the drive.

4. Insert a diskette into the drive if you have not already done so, close the diskette drive door on 5 ¼-inch drives, and press ↵Enter.

Format checks the existing diskette format. If the diskette has never been formatted, nothing needs to be checked, and the program formats the diskette. If it has been formatted, DOS saves the existing format information, which you can use to unformat the diskette later. As the diskette is formatted, the percentage of the diskette that has been formatted is displayed. When the formatting process is complete, you see the following message:

```
Format complete.
Volume label (11 characters, ENTER for none)?
```

5. Type a volume label and press ⏎Enter, or just press ⏎Enter for no label.

   DOS reserves a few bytes of space on diskettes so that you can place an electronic identifier, called a volume label, on each diskette. Think of a volume label for a diskette in the same context as the title of a book. When you assign a volume label, you can use the following characters, in any order:

   - Letters A to Z and a to z
   - Numerals 0 to 9
   - Special characters and punctuation symbols:

     ~ ! @ # $ ^ & ( ) _ { } `

   If you try to enter too many characters, you hear a beep after the 11th character. If you enter an illegal character, you see an error message and a prompt to enter the volume label again. If you do not want to name the diskette, press ⏎Enter without typing a name.

6. DOS displays detailed information about the formatted diskette and then asks whether you want to format another diskette. Press N and ⏎Enter if you do not want to format any more diskettes. Press Y and ⏎Enter if you want to format another diskette.

7. When you are done formatting, press any key to return to the Shell.

Formatting Different Types of Disks

At times, DOS might not know what type of diskette you want to format. If you have a 5 ¼-inch, 360K drive or a 3 ½-inch, 720K drive, you have no problems. These drives can use only one type of diskette, so DOS always knows what type of diskette is in the drive.

High-capacity diskette drives can format more than one type of diskette. If you have a 1.2M drive, you can use either 360K or 1.2M diskettes. If you have a 1.44M drive, you can use either 720K or 1.44M diskettes. In some cases, you must specify the diskette type in the Format dialog box. The default type of diskette is always the highest-capacity diskette that can work in the drive.

When you format a new diskette in a 1.2M drive, DOS assumes that it is a 1.2M diskette, unless you tell it otherwise. So if you want to format a 1.2M diskette in a 1.2M drive, you do not have to do anything special. If you want to format a 360K diskette in a 1.2M drive, however, you must tell DOS the diskette type. You specify the diskette type in the Parameters text box in the Format dialog box.

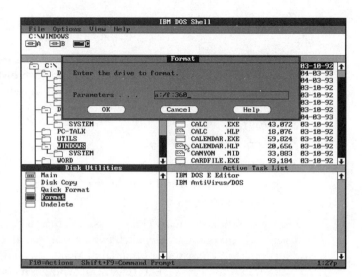

The information in this Parameters text box says to format a 360K disk in drive A. The /F: parameter is known as a size switch; however, it specifies the capacity of the disk, not its size. A *switch* is special information that gives instructions to a command.

5

Before you type the size parameter, you must clear the highlight in the text box. If you begin typing without clearing the highlight, the current parameter (a:) disappears. Press the End key or click the mouse pointer at the end of the parameter to cancel the highlight.

To specify the size, first type a slash (/) to let DOS know that a command switch follows. The size switch is /F: followed by the capacity of the diskette. In this case, you would type **/F:360**.

To format a 720K diskette in a 1.44M drive, use the switch **/F:720**. To format a diskette in drive B, do not press End to clear the highlight, just type **b:** followed by the switch.

Looking at the FORMAT Command's Output

After the format is complete and you type a volume label and press Enter, you see a report of the status of the diskette. The report shows the total disk space and total bytes available on the diskette. If FORMAT detects *bad sectors* on the diskette, it marks them as unusable. FORMAT also reports how many bytes are unavailable because of bad sectors. Other information includes how many bytes each *allocation unit* contains, how many allocation units are available on the diskette for storage, and the volume serial number that DOS automatically assigns to every diskette. An allocation unit is a group of sectors that DOS uses to keep track of where files are on a diskette.

The numbers for various sizes of diskettes vary, as shown in the following figures.

```
Insert new diskette for drive A:
and press ENTER when ready...

Checking existing disk format.
Saving UNFORMAT information.
Verifying 1.2M
Format complete.

Volume label (11 characters, ENTER for none)?

   1213952 bytes total disk space
     15360 bytes in bad sectors
   1198592 bytes available on disk

       512 bytes in each allocation unit.
      2341 allocation units available on disk.

Volume Serial Number is 262D-14E8

Format another (Y/N)?
```

This report shows diskette information for a 1.2M diskette with bad sectors.

```
Insert new diskette for drive B:
and press ENTER when ready...

Checking existing disk format.
Saving UNFORMAT information.
Verifying 720K
Format complete.

Volume label (11 characters, ENTER for none)?

    730112 bytes total disk space
    730112 bytes available on disk

      1024 bytes in each allocation unit.
       713 allocation units available on disk.

Volume Serial Number is 3F1B-14F0

Format another (Y/N)?
```

This report shows diskette information for a 720K diskette.

5

Quick Formatting

If a diskette has been formatted before, you can clear the entire diskette quickly by using the *quick format.* When you format a diskette, DOS lays out the sectors, checks every track for bad sectors, and builds the directory and file allocation table. If the diskette has been formatted before, you can skip most of this work and just clear the directory and file allocation table in a few seconds. You do not have to specify which type of diskette is in the drive because DOS can determine the diskette type from the previous format. To perform a quick format, choose Quick Format from the Disk Utilities program group.

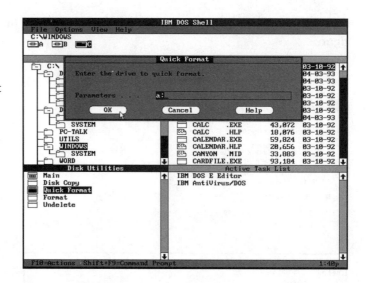

The Quick Format dialog box opens. A Quick Format proceeds just like a regular format except that it takes only a few seconds.

5

If it can, DOS saves the existing format information during a Quick Format the same way it saves it during a regular format. Still, you should take care not to Quick Format a disk that has important information on it.

Understanding FORMAT's Error Messages

The most common DOS error messages that occur during diskette formatting are rarely catastrophes. They are little more than statements suggesting that you did something wrong or that DOS had trouble carrying out the command. For example, if you reformat a completely full diskette, there is no room to save the information that would allow the diskette to be unformatted. You see a warning message that the diskette cannot be unformatted. If you try to format a write-protected diskette, for example, you see a message indicating that the format cannot be completed.

The following sections describe three common formatting error messages.

Not Ready

If you respond to the Press any key when ready prompt without placing a disk in the disk drive, or if the drive door is open, DOS displays the message:

```
Not ready
Format another (Y/N)?
```

Just insert the diskette, close the door if necessary, press Y and Enter to start the format. If you specified the wrong diskette drive, press N and Enter. Then issue the command again with the correct drive letter.

```
Insert new diskette for drive A:
and press ENTER when ready...

Checking existing disk format.
Not ready
QuickFormat another (Y/N)?
```

This message means that DOS cannot read from the diskette drive.

If the diskette is in the drive and the drive door is closed and you get this error, the diskette is probably write-protected. Take the diskette out and check the write-protect tab.

To format a write-protected diskette, remove the write-protect tape from a 5 ¼-inch diskette or slide the tab on a 3 ½-inch diskette, reinsert the diskette, and press Y and Enter at the prompt.

5

Bad Sectors

Although not a true error message, a bad-sectors report points out a possible problem with the diskette.

```
Insert new diskette for drive A:
and press ENTER when ready...

Checking existing disk format.
Saving UNFORMAT information.
Verifying 1.2M
Format complete.

Volume label (11 characters, ENTER for none)?

    1213952 bytes total disk space
      15360 bytes in bad sectors
    1198592 bytes available on disk

        512 bytes in each allocation unit.
       2341 allocation units available on disk.

Volume Serial Number is 3D21-14F6

Format another (Y/N)?
```

If the FORMAT command detects unusable areas on the diskette, you see a line describing the problem in the report.

The bytes in bad sectors message means that DOS found bad sectors on the diskette. These sectors cannot be used to hold information. The total amount of free space on the diskette is reduced by the number of bytes in the bad sectors.

Try reformatting the diskette. If it still has bad sectors and is a new diskette, you can have your dealer replace the diskette, or you can use the diskette as is. Before you do either, though, try formatting the diskette again.

If you get a very large number of bad sectors, you may have tried to format a 360K diskette as a 1.2M diskette. DOS tries to format the diskette, but after the computer grinds and chugs, you end up with mostly bad sectors. Format the diskette again with the /F:360 switch.

Disk Unusable

The worst disk-error message you can get is the following:

```
Invalid media or Track 0 bad   disk unusable
```

5

This disk may have a scratched surface; DOS couldn't read information on the first track.

```
Insert new diskette for drive B:
and press ENTER when ready...

Checking existing disk format.
Formatting 1.44M
Invalid media or Track 0 bad - disk unusable.
Format terminated.
Format another (Y/N)?
```

You may receive this error message for two possible reasons. If you try to format a 720K diskette as a 1.44M diskette, you will get this message. Format the diskette again with the /F:720 switch.

This message also can mean that the areas on the diskette that hold important DOS system data are bad. If you get the disk unusable error message on a new diskette, take it back to your dealer. If the diskette is old, throw it away. Diskettes are inexpensive and, in this case, should be discarded. Trying to use a bad diskette is being penny-wise and pound-foolish.

Cautions about Formatting a Hard Disk

Hard disks are a desirable part of a computer system because of their speed and storage capacity. Just like diskettes, you must format them before you use them. Unless you are familiar with the procedure, however, *do not attempt to format your hard disk.*

Many computer dealers install the operating system on a computer's hard disk before you receive it. If your dealer has installed an applications program, such as a word processor, *do not* format the hard disk. If you reformat your hard disk, you will erase all programs and data.

Should you ever attempt to reformat your hard disk, first perform a complete backup. You also should have a bootable diskette ready that contains a copy of the DOS Backup program.

Remember that the FORMAT command erases all the data a disk contains. Always check the directory of the diskette you want to format; it may hold data you need. Check the command line thoroughly when you use the FORMAT command.

Reformatting Disks

You can use either Format or Quick Format to reformat a previously formatted diskette. You should be very careful about reformatting diskettes, however. Always check the directory listing of the diskette before reformatting it to be sure there are no important files on it.

When you format a diskette that has been formatted previously, DOS saves some information that allows you to *unformat* the diskette. Remember, when you format a diskette, you tell DOS to completely clear the diskette so that you can use it again; however, DOS saves the information that was on the diskette. If you format a diskette in error and do not put any other files on the diskette, you can use the UNFORMAT command from the command line to unformat the diskette and recover these files.

```
Insert new diskette for drive A:
and press ENTER when ready...

Checking existing disk format.
Saving UNFORMAT information.
Verifying 1.2M
Format complete.

Volume label (11 characters, ENTER for none)?
```

When you reformat a previously formatted diskette, DOS saves the information on the diskette so that you can unformat the diskette and recover the data.

93

In some cases, DOS cannot save the unformat information and warns you that the diskette cannot be unformatted.

```
Insert new diskette for drive B:
and press ENTER when ready...

Checking existing disk format.
Existing format differs from that specified.
This disk cannot be unformatted.
Proceed with Format (Y/N)?
```

You can proceed with the format with no hope of recovering the data, or you can cancel the Format command.

Duplicating Disks

One instance when it is not necessary to format a diskette before using it is with the Disk Copy command. Disk Copy lets you make an exact duplicate of a diskette by copying all the files, directories, and diskette information from an existing diskette onto a new one.

Disk Copy, like Format, is in the Disk Utilities program group. When you use Disk Copy, DOS issues the DISKCOPY command to make an exact copy of a diskette. DOS reads the original, or source, diskette, and then writes the data to the destination, or target, diskette. If the destination diskette has not been formatted, DOS will format it during the Disk Copy. If the destination has been formatted, and it contains files, all the files will be lost.

Disk Copy creates a duplicate of an entire diskette. Both the source diskette and the destination diskette must be the same size and capacity. You cannot use Disk Copy to duplicate a 5 ¼-inch diskette onto a 3 ½-inch diskette, or vice versa.

If you have two diskette drives that are the same size, using Disk Copy is a breeze. Simply place your source diskette into drive A, the source drive, and the destination diskette into drive B, the destination drive.

If you have only one diskette drive, or if you have two different size diskette drives, you must use the same diskette drive for both the source and the destination diskettes. DOS tells you when to insert the source diskette and when to insert the destination diskette by displaying a message on your screen as it performs the Disk Copy.

To perform a Disk Copy, follow these steps:

1. Open the Disk Utilities program group if it is not already open.

2. Select Disk Copy. The Disk Copy dialog box is displayed.

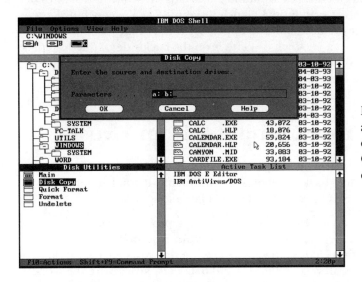

Enter the source and destination drives and press OK to begin the copy process.

3. Enter the source and target diskette drives in the Parameters text box. If your drives are the same size, type **a: b:**. If you have only one drive, type **a: a:**. If you have different size drives, select the one that the diskette you want to copy fits in, and enter that as both the source and destination drive.

4. Select OK.

   DOS prompts you to insert the required diskettes in the selected drives.

5. When the copy is complete, DOS asks if you want to copy another diskette. Type Y and press Enter if you want to copy another. Type N and press Enter if you do not. Press any key to return to the PC DOS Shell.

Write-Protecting Disks

It is important to know how to protect the files on your diskettes from being overwritten. You should label the diskettes so that you know what is stored on each one. You should always do a directory of a diskette before performing any action on it. And you should try to be very careful with potentially devastating commands such as FORMAT and DISKCOPY.

Another precaution is to write-protect diskettes that hold important information. You write-protect a diskette by adding tape tabs on 5 ¼-inch diskettes or setting the write-protect switch on 3 ½-inch diskettes. On a 5 ¼-inch diskette, put the tape tab over the notch on the upper-right side of the diskette. The write-protect switch on a 3 ½-inch diskette is on the back-side of the diskette's upper-right corner. To set the switch, slide it up so that the window is open. When the window is closed, write-protection is off.

Protecting Your Computer from Viruses

5

Once you have formatted your diskettes, they are ready for use. You can store data on them, including backed up files and programs. If you keep them in a safe place, and exercise precautions, they will last a long time.

However, problems can arise. One type of software problem that can affect your diskettes and cause serious data loss is a *virus*. A computer virus is a set of computer instructions hidden inside a program that can take over your computer and destroy all your programs and data files. Viruses are the work of computer vandals who destroy the property of others for "fun."

A virus rarely infects commercial software. Viruses usually are found in free software distributed through electronic bulletin board systems (BBSs) and passed around on diskettes. Operators of bulletin board systems work very hard to avoid viruses, but the risk is not completely eliminated.

To practice "safe computing," never use a program from someone you do not know. Before you use any program, talk with others who have used the program and make sure that they have had no problems. Also make sure that the date and file size of both versions of the program are identical. Two "copies" of what should be the same program with different sizes is a clue that the larger one is infected with a virus.

Another way to help protect your computer from viruses is to keep good, up-to-date backups available. Sometimes, the only way to clean up an infected system is to restore it using a virus-free backup.

Unfortunately, viruses are becoming all too common. Fortunately, there are anti-virus protection programs you can use to detect and remove viruses from your computer. PC DOS 6 includes a powerful anti-virus program: IBM AntiVirus/DOS. AntiVirus can prevent, detect and remove computer viruses. It can work in the background, automatically providing protection at all times, or you can use it to check selected diskettes and hard disks for viruses.

Using AntiVirus/DOS

AntiVirus/DOS is loaded if selected during setup and installation. It appears in the Shell in the Main program group in the Program Area.

To start AntiVirus, open the Main program group, if it is not already open, and select the IBM AntiVirus/DOS program icon. The AntiVirus main screen appears.

AntiVirus uses a shell similar to the DOS Shell. You can use the keyboard or the mouse to make selections from menus or dialog boxes. In addition, the program displays a list of shortcut keys along the bottom of your screen. With a mouse, you can click on the word. Select F1 to display context-sensitive help screens; select F2 to display help about the shortcut keys; select F3 to exit back to the DOS Shell.

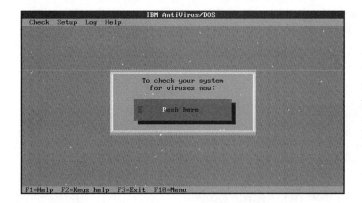

To scan the current drive for viruses, press P, or click on the Push here box.

Use the Check menu to check a diskette or diskette drive other than the current drive.

AntiVirus lets you perform *automated checking,* which checks your disks for viruses whenever you boot your system, You can set automated checking for daily, weekly, monthly or no checks using the Setup menu.

If automated checking detects a virus, you will be prompted to perform a thorough examination of your computer in order to find every instance of the virus and to remove it.

AntiVirus also offers *DOS Shielding,* which checks DOS memory for viruses whenever you start DOS and monitors programs as you run them in DOS. DOS Shielding disables viruses and prevents them from becoming active or spreading. You can change the DOS Shielding settings using the Setup menu.

AntiVirus keeps logs of the checks it performs so that you can review them later. The logs contain information about the date of the check, the files that were checked, and whether or not any viruses were found. Use the Log menu to look at the information AntiVirus gathered during the current scan, during the previous scan, and accumulated from every scan ever performed.

The Help menu lets you select from a list of context-sensitive help topics or displays a list of known viruses.

As AntiVirus scans a disk, it displays a status window showing you how much memory is being scanned and how many directories and files are being scanned.

To interrupt the scan, press Esc, click on the Stop button, or press *s*.

When the scan is complete, AntiVirus provides you with information on any viruses found, and prompts you to take action to remove them. Choose OK or click the close box at the top left corner of the window to return to the main AntiVirus screen.

When you have finished using AntiVirus, press F3 to return to the DOS Shell.

Lessons Learned

- Different types of diskettes and diskette drives are available.
- You have to match the diskettes you buy to the diskette drive in your computer.
- You can give your diskettes electronic labels.
- You can "quick format" a previously formatted diskette in a few seconds.
- Error messages can be helpful. Most of them do not indicate an impending catastrophe.
- Hard disks demand special treatment and care when you use the FORMAT command.
- When you reformat a diskette that has already been formatted, DOS saves the UNFORMAT information.
- You can use Disk Copy to make an exact duplicate of a diskette, without formatting the new diskette first.
- You can protect your computer system from software viruses using IBM AntiVirus/DOS.

In the next chapter, you learn how to manage your hard disk and its directories.

Using Your Hard Disk and Directories

6

Before the oil crisis of the 1970s, you could stop at any service station and pick up a free map. In fact, one oil company even provided travel routes. All you did was write to a special address and tell the oil company where you planned to go. Within a few weeks, a map arrived showing both the quickest and the most scenic routes. DOS's directory structure provides something resembling that kind of personal touch.

Understanding the DOS directory concept

Navigating a hard disk's directories

Finding paths in the tree structure

Viewing directories

Exploring sample subdirectories

Managing a hard disk drive

Viewing directories and file information

Key Terms Used in This Chapter	
Hierarchical directory	An organizational structure used by DOS to separate files into levels of subdirectories.
Tree structure	A term applied to hierarchical directories to describe the concept in which directories "belong" to higher directories and "own" lower directories. Viewed graphically, the ownership relationships resemble an inverted tree.
Directory	An area of the DOS file system that holds information about files and directories. The root directory is the highest directory of DOS's tree structure. All DOS disks have a root directory, which DOS creates automatically.
Subdirectory	A directory created within another directory and subordinate to that directory. Also called, simply, a directory.
Directory specifier	A DOS command parameter that tells DOS where to find a file or where to carry out a command.
Path name	Another name for the directory specifier. The path name gives DOS the necessary directions to trace the directory tree to the directory that contains the desired commands or files.
Backslash (\)	The character used in commands to separate directory names. Used alone as a parameter, the backslash signifies the root, or highest directory.

Understanding the DOS Directory Concept

DOS doesn't strand you on the road without a map. Understandably, people beginning to use a PC don't know the "proper address" to write for the scenic or direct routes. This chapter is designed to be your map to DOS.

In earlier chapters, you saw file lists of the contents of a disk directory. You learned to use DIR from the command line to display a directory, and you learned that the DOS Shell displays a directory in the Directory Tree area.

A directory is more than a file list displayed on-screen. It also is part of an internal software listing that DOS stores in a magnetic index on the disk. A poorly structured disk directory turns any hard drive into a bewildering tangle of misplaced files.

This chapter explains DOS's hierarchical directory structure. You discover how to use DOS to group and organize files. You also learn how DOS commands can help you organize your disk directories logically.

Navigating a Hard Disk's Directories

DOS uses directories to organize files on a disk. A directory listing contains file information—the name, size, and creation or revision date for each file. Computer operators use the directory of a disk to find specific files. DOS also uses some or all of this directory information to service requests for data stored in the files on disks.

All DOS-based disks have at least one directory. One directory usually is adequate for a diskette. Because diskettes have relatively limited capacities, the number of files that fit on a diskette is limited. Hard disks, on the other hand, have very large storage capacities. A hard disk can contain hundreds or even thousands of files. Without some form of organization, you will waste time sifting and sorting through your disk's directories to find a specific file.

Although diskettes can use DOS's multiple directory structure, this feature is more important for extending order to the storage capacity of hard disks. DOS incorporates the hierarchical directory system. This term means that one directory leads to another, which can lead to another, and so on. This multi-level file structure enables you to create a filing system. With a bit of foresight, you can store your files in logically grouped directories so that you (and DOS) can locate your files more easily.

The term *tree structure* describes the organization of files into hierarchical levels of directories. Try picturing the tree structure as an inverted tree. You can visualize the file system with the first-level directory as the root or trunk of the tree. The trunk branches into major limbs to the next level of directories under the root. These directories branch into other directories. Directories have files, like leaves, attached to them.

6

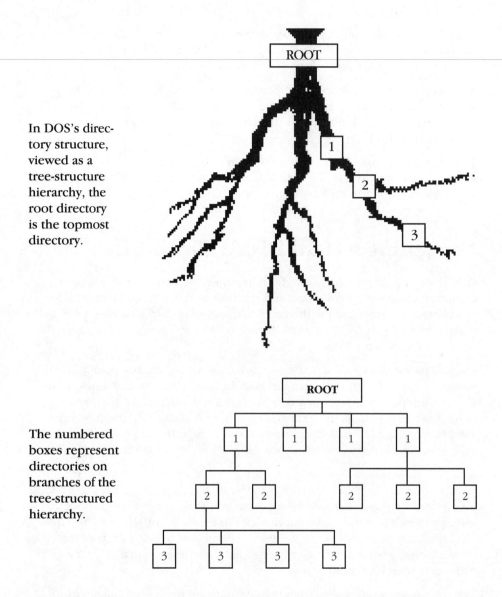

In DOS's directory structure, viewed as a tree-structure hierarchy, the root directory is the topmost directory.

6

The numbered boxes represent directories on branches of the tree-structured hierarchy.

When you format a diskette, DOS creates a main directory for that diskette. This directory is called the *root directory.* The root directory is the default directory until you change to another directory. DOS designates the root directory with the backslash (\) character. You cannot delete the root directory.

A *subdirectory* is any directory, excluding the root directory. A subdirectory can contain data files as well as other subdirectories. Subdirectory names must conform to the rules for naming DOS files, but subdirectory names normally do not have extensions. You should name subdirectories for the type of files they contain so that you will remember what type of files each subdirectory contains.

The terms *directory* and *subdirectory* frequently are used interchangeably. A subdirectory of the root can have its own subdirectories. By naming the branches, you can describe where you are working in the tree structure. You simply start at the root and name each branch that leads to your current branch. Directories also are frequently called "parent" and "child" directories. Each child of the parent can have "children" of its own. In the directory hierarchy, each directory's parent is the directory just above it.

Any directory, except the root, can have as many subdirectories as space on the disk permits. Depending on the disk drive, the root directory can handle a preset number of subdirectories. In the $5\,^1/_4$-inch size, 360K diskettes hold 112 entries and 1.2M diskettes handle 224 entries in the root directory. In the $3\,^1/_2$-inch size, 720K and 1.4M diskettes can hold, respectively, 112 and 224 entries. Hard disks have a typical root directory capacity of 512 entries.

Directories do not share information about their contents with other directories. In a way, each subdirectory acts as a disk within a bigger disk. This idea of privacy extends to the DOS commands you issue. The directory structure permits DOS commands to act on the contents of the current directory and leave other directories undisturbed.

When you issue a command that specifies a file but not a directory, DOS looks for that file in the current directory. You can access any point in the tree structure and remain at your current directory.

Any squirrel knows that you cannot reach the farthest branch of a limb without starting from the limb nearest the base. From there, the limb branches off to several others. The important thing to note is that you cannot use more than one limb to reach any of the limb's potentially numerous branches. Consider a directory path as the series of limbs you must travel on the way to a particular destination branch.

Finding Paths in the Tree Structure

Before DOS can locate a file in the tree structure, it must know where to find the file. The *directory specifier* simply tells DOS the directory in which a certain file resides. DOS must know the drive that you want to use, the directory name, and the name of the file.

To specify the directory from the Shell, you first select the disk drive, then the directory, then the file. To specify the directory from the command line, you type the disk drive, the directory name, and finally, the filename. DOS uses this information to find and act on the file.

Path Names

You can compare DOS to a corporate empire that has an extremely strict order of command. All communications must "go through channels." If a subsidiary at level 3 wants to communicate with the parent corporation, for example, the message must go through subsidiaries 2 and 1. In DOS, this routing is called a *path*.

6

The parent corporation is analogous to the root directory, and the subsidiaries are analogous to subdirectories.

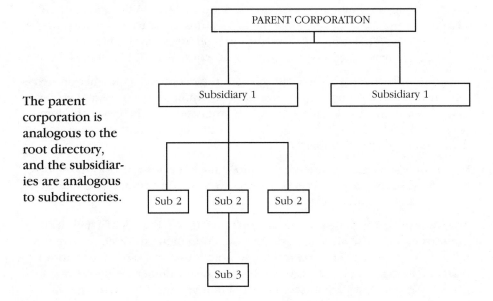

A *path name* is a chain of directory names that tells DOS how to find the file that you want. You must build complete path names when you use the DOS prompt. When you use the Shell, the paths are supplied visually in the Directory Tree area. If you understand paths now, you can easily use the command line later.

To create a path name chain, you type the drive name, a subdirectory name (or sequence of subdirectory names), and the filename. Make sure that you separate subdirectory names from each other with a *backslash* (\\) character. Using symbolic notation, the path name looks like the following:

d:\\directory\\directory…\\filename.ext

In this notation, *d:* is the drive letter. If you fail to specify the drive, DOS uses the current drive.

directory\\directory… is the directory specifier. It names the directories you want to search. The ellipsis (…) simply means that you can add other directories to the specifier list. If you omit the directory specifier from the path name, DOS assumes that you want to use the current directory.

filename.ext is the name of the file. Notice that you use a backslash (\\) to separate directory names and the filename. The path name fully describes to DOS where to direct its search for the file.

Use the following simple directory setup to understand directory paths in DOS. Each subdirectory in this sample is a subdirectory of the root directory.

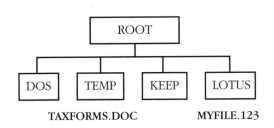

The subdirectory TEMP has a file called TAXFORMS.DOC, and the subdirectory LOTUS has a file called MYFILE.123.

The complete path name for the MYFILE.123 file is the chain of directories that tells DOS how to find MYFILE.123. In this case, the chain consists of just two directories: the root (\\) and LOTUS. The path name is

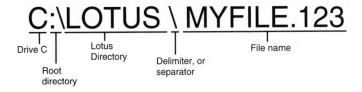

105

The path name for the TAXFORMS.DOC file is

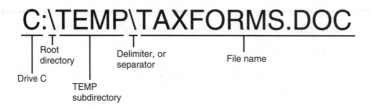

The Search's Starting Point

When you type a path name, DOS searches in the first specified directory. It then passes through the other specified directory branches to the file. The root directory is represented by the backslash (\) instead of a directory name. If you want the search path to start at the root directory, from which all directories grow, begin the directory specification with a \. DOS then begins its search for the file in the root and follows the subdirectory chain you included in the command.

Suppose that you want to see the directory listing for a budget file you created with your Lotus 1-2-3 program. You might use the DIR command to give DOS a path similar to the following:

DIR C:\LOTUS\DATA\BUDGET.WK1

DOS searches on drive C, beginning with the root directory, proceeds to the LOTUS subdirectory, and then arrives at the DATA subdirectory, where it finds the Budget.Wk1 file.

If you omit the \ root name designator, the search starts in your current directory, not the root directory. DOS uses the path to your current directory as its default. If the current directory doesn't lead to the subdirectory that contains the file, the error message File not found appears on-screen. If the current directory contains the subdirectory, however, you do not have to type all the directory names in the path. Using the preceding example, if the current directory is C:\LOTUS, you can see the listing for the budget file by typing the following command at the DOS prompt:

DIR DATA\BUDGET.WK1

6

Viewing the Directory Structure

The illustrations in the last chapter depicted some rather complex hard disk directory structures. This section starts with some simple directory structures using drive A. Although drive A is used here as a sample, directory structures are rarely used on diskettes. They are more applicable to hard disks.

A variety of arrangements for the directory structure is possible. This sample structure has four subdirectories under the root, or A:\, directory.

Many times, a second level of directories is useful. For example, you might want to group a series of related program directories under one directory, or group a number of data directories under one directory. Many people find that two levels of subdirectories are sufficient.

When you see a plus sign in a file folder icon for a directory, you can expand the directory listing to see the subdirectories for that directory. To use the mouse to expand a single directory, click on the plus sign. To use the keyboard to expand a single directory, select that directory and press the plus (+) key. To expand all the directories in the directory tree, choose Expand **All** from the Tree menu, or press Ctrl-* (asterisk).

This sample directory structure has two levels of directories under the root. Only the first level appears. If a directory has additional levels of subdirectories under it, a plus sign (+) appears in the file folder icon.

When the directories are expanded, you can see that the DATA directory has three subdirectories and TEMP has one.

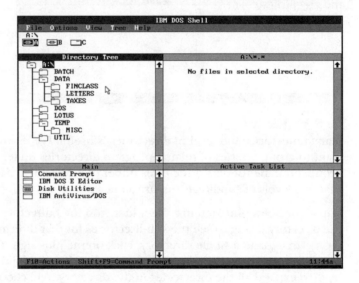

When you see a minus sign (–) in a file folder icon for a directory, you can collapse that directory's listing to hide the subdirectories. To use the mouse to collapse a single directory, click on the minus sign. To use the keyboard to collapse a single directory, select that directory and press the minus (–) key.

Exploring Sample Subdirectories

Although you may not know exactly what kind of directory organization you need, now is a good time to give some thought to establishing your directory tree. Use the following sample directories to help you decide what directories you want to build on your hard disk. If your computer is part of a network, check with the network administrator before you make any changes.

The Root Directory

DOS creates the root directory for you, but you control which files to include in the root. As a general rule, you should avoid cluttering the root directory of a hard disk with files.

Because the root is the default directory for DOS when you boot your system, you must include COMMAND.COM in the root directory of your first hard disk and any diskette that you use to boot your computer. COMMAND.COM is the DOS command processor. DOS expects to find COMMAND.COM in the current directory when you boot. If DOS cannot find COMMAND.COM and load it, it cannot communicate with you. All it can do is warn you that it cannot find the command interpreter.

In addition to COMMAND.COM, the root directory probably contains AUTOEXEC.BAT and CONFIG.SYS files. DOS uses these files when you boot the computer. Almost all other files should find a home in another appropriate subdirectory.

6

The \DOS Directory

When you install DOS on your hard disk, the installation procedure creates the \DOS directory (and \DOS\SYSTEM and \DOS\DATA subdirectories) and copies the DOS files into this directory. Never place any files in the \DOS directory except DOS files.

The \UTIL or \UTILITY Directory

Just as you keep all your DOS files in the \DOS directory, you may want to keep utility programs in their own directory. Most people accumulate a variety of small utility programs such as print spoolers, mouse drivers, file compression utilities, disk utilities, and so on. If you keep them in the \UTIL or \UTILITY directory you will always know where to find them.

Do not place utility programs in the \DOS directory. If you upgrade your version of DOS later, these programs may be deleted.

Applications Software Directories

Many applications packages, such as Lotus 1-2-3, create directories when you install them on your hard disk. If a program doesn't create a directory, you should create one with a name that suggests the software name. For example, you might name your spreadsheet directory LOTUS. You can then copy the 1-2-3 package's files to that directory.

If you work with multiple versions of the same program, you might name a subdirectory 123R24 for the 1-2-3 Release 2.4 program files and 123R31 for the 1-2-3 Release 3.1 program files. If you have enough disk space, you should keep both the old version and the new version of a program available for a while in case you have problems with the new version.

The \DATA Directory

You probably use your personal computer for many different applications. Therefore, you create many different data files. Some people create a data subdirectory under each program directory. If they have a \LOTUS directory with the 1-2-3 program files, for example, they create a \LOTUS\DATA or \LOTUS\FILES directory for worksheet files.

This structure works, but there is a better one. Create a directory called \DATA, and then create subdirectories for each project or application. For example, you would put all the files related to your taxes in the \DATA\TAXES directory. If you take a class in finance, you could put all the homework assignments in the \DATA\FINCLASS directory. The \DATA\FINCLASS directory might contain both worksheet files and word processing files, but they are all related to one activity.

With a \DATA directory, you can back up all your data easily without making a backup copy of your programs. All you have to do is backup your \DATA directory.

The \TEMP Directory

Many users find that they need a directory to store temporary files. You might find a directory named \TEMP useful. You can copy files to \TEMP as a temporary storage place until you copy the files to a more appropriate directory.

A \TEMP directory also is useful for making copies of diskettes in a single diskette drive, low-memory system. You can copy files from the source disk to the \TEMP directory and then copy them back to the destination disk. If you have a single diskette drive, this copy method keeps you from swapping disks in and out of the single drive.

Do not use the \TEMP directory as a permanent home for a file, however. You should be able to erase all the files in this directory periodically so that you can keep the \TEMP directory empty for later use.

The \MISC or \KEEP Directory

You may have files in different directories that are no longer active, but that you may still need. Inactive files in a directory tend to increase clutter and make sorting through the directory confusing. With a \MISC or a \KEEP directory, you have an easily remembered home for those inactive files.

The \BATCH Directory

Batch files are text files that contain DOS commands and start programs. You can place many commands in one batch file. Even if you use the Shell to run commands and programs, you will probably use batch files. Most users keep their batch files in a separate \BATCH directory.

6

Managing a Hard Disk Drive

The examples presented so far in this chapter provide information on the structure of hierarchical directories. The following commands relate to your directory system's maintenance and use. With directory commands, you can customize your file system and navigate through it.

Creating a New Directory

To make a new directory in the Shell, follow these steps:

1. Select the parent directory where you want to add a subdirectory. For example, if you want to add a subdirectory to the root, select the root directory.

2. Select Create Directory from the File menu to create a new directory under the selected directory. The Create Directory dialog box appears.

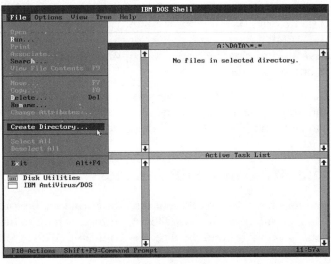

Making a new
directory with the
Create Directory
command.

3. Type the name of the new directory in the text box. A directory name
   must be a valid filename of one to eight characters and may have an
   extension of up to three characters.

6

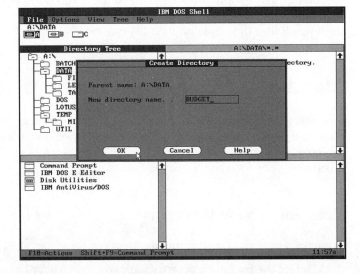

In this example,
the new directory
name is BUDGET.

4. Choose OK.

112

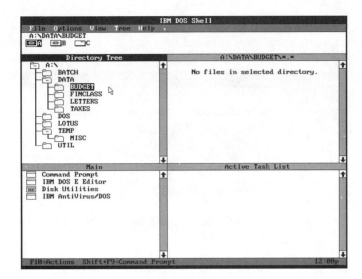

\DATA\BUDGET
is added to the
directory tree.

As soon as you create a new directory, it appears in the Directory Tree area.

Changing the Current Directory

The directory selected in the Directory Tree is the *current directory*. The files for the current directory are listed in the Files area to the right of the Directory Tree. Generally, the term "current" is used when you use the command line instead of the Shell. The term "selected" is more appropriate to the Shell.

To use the mouse to change the current, or selected, directory, click another directory name. To use the keyboard to change the current directory, press the Tab key until you select the Directory Tree area, and then use the down-arrow and up-arrow keys to select the directory you want.

If the directory you want to select is a subdirectory of another directory and does not appear on the Directory Tree, expand the Directory Tree and then select the subdirectory.

Removing a Directory

Before you remove a directory using the DOS Shell, you must first delete all the files stored in the unwanted directory, or move them to another directory. To delete a file, select it in the Files area and then choose **Delete** from the File menu or press the Del key. Choose Yes in the Delete File Confirmation dialog box.

113

To remove an empty directory, first select the directory. Then choose **Delete** from the File menu or, as a shortcut, press the Del key.

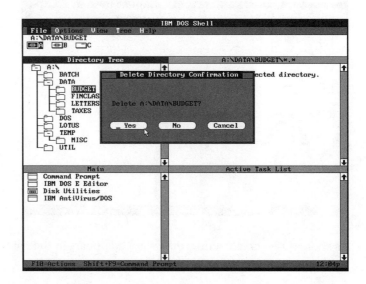

When you delete a directory, a confirmation dialog box appears. Choose Yes to remove the directory; choose No or Cancel if you do not want to remove it.

If you try to delete a directory that has one or more subdirectories or contains files, the Deletion Error dialog box appears.

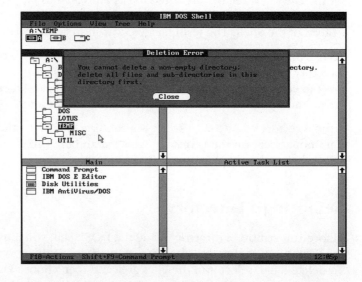

Because the selected directory, TEMP, has a subdirectory, MISC, you cannot delete TEMP until you first delete MISC. Select the Close button to clear the Deletion Error dialog box and cancel the command.

Viewing Directories

The standard file list displays all the files in the selected directory in order by filename.

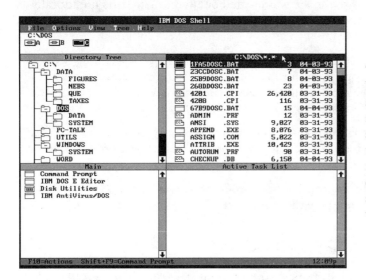

The Files area title bar indicates the selected directory and the file specification. In this case, C:\DOS is the selected directory. To specify all files, use *.*.

You can change this file list display in two ways. First, you can change the order in which DOS displays the files; or, if you want to see only specific files from a directory with many files, you can change the type of files DOS displays. You use the File Display Options dialog box to accomplish both of these tasks.

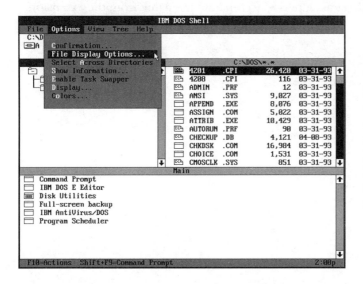

To access the File Display Options dialog box and change the display of the file lists, choose File Display Options from the Options menu.

Changing the Sort Order

You can sort files according to five sort options. *Name* sorts alphabetically by filename. *Extension* sorts alphabetically by filename extension. *Date* sorts numerically by the date the file was created or altered. *Size* sorts numerically by file size. *DiskOrder* sorts according to where the files are stored on the disk.

You also have two additional options. You can select the Descending order box to reverse the sort order; for instance, you select this box to list files that begin with the letter *Z* before those that begin with *A*. And you can select the Display hidden/system files box to display those files.

Note: If you are updating many files in a large directory, you may want to list the files by date instead of by name, or by date in descending order so that you can easily tell which files are new.

After you choose the appropriate sort order in the File Display Options dialog box, choose OK to complete the command.

Changing the File Specification

The *file specification* tells DOS what files to display. The default *.* file specification displays files with any filename and any file extension. The asterisk is a *wildcard* that matches any number of characters in the filename or extension.

To change a file specification, simply type a file specification in the Name text box in the File Display Options dialog box. When you enter a file specification, you must enter a filename, a period to separate the name from the extension, and an extension.

6

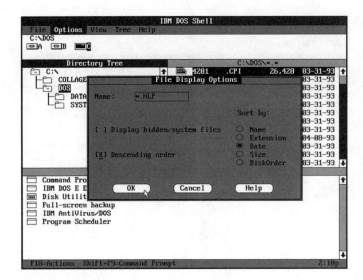

In the File Display Options dialog box, enter the file specifier in the Name: text box. Select the sort order you want in the Sort by: area. Choose Descending order if applicable.

The following table shows some sample file specifications that contain the asterisk wildcard:

File Specification	Files Displayed
.	All files
*.BAS	All files with a BAS extension
*.DOC	All files with a DOC extension
.WK	All files with an extension that begins with WK, such as WKS or WK1
BUDGET.*	All files with the name BUDGET and any extension
TAX199*.*	All files with a name that starts with TAX199 and any extension, such as TAX1991.DOC, TAX1992.WK1, or TAX199.TXT

In most cases, you will want to display all files with a certain file extension.

6

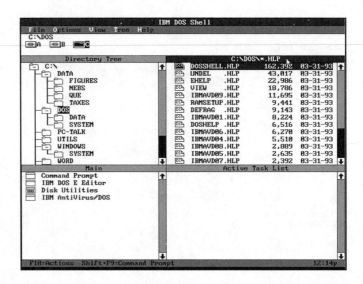

This Files area title bar shows that only files with the HLP extension are displayed. The sort is by size, in descending order.

The selective file display can be even more powerful when you want to look at all the files on a disk in one display. You can display files with a certain file extension, regardless of where they are located on the disk. This option can help you find misplaced files or the names of files you have forgotten.

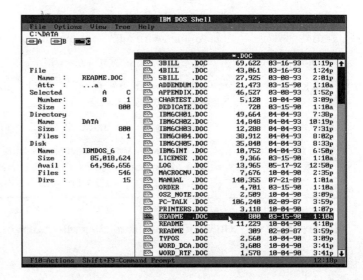

In this example, all files with the file extension DOC are displayed.

This is the result of using File Display Options to display files with the file specification *.DOC and changing the View option to All Files. Detailed file information on the selected file appears on the left. The disk contains three files with the name README.DOC. The selected file is in the \DATA directory. To find the location of the other README.DOC files, select them and read the file information for that file.

Displaying File Information

When you set the View option to All Files, detailed file information for the selected file appears to the left of the file list. To display this information in the other views, select the file and choose Show Information from the Options menu.

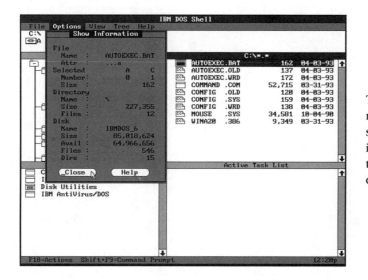

The Show Information dialog box shows detailed information about the selected disk, directory, and file.

You see the selected file, the selected directory, the total size of the directory, the number of files in the directory, the disk label of the selected disk, total size of the disk, number of bytes available on the disk, and the number of files on the disk.

119

Lessons Learned

■ You can use DOS's hierarchical directory system to organize your files so that they are easy to find.

■ The path concept is essentially the mapping out of a course for DOS to search.

■ The root directory is the beginning directory. All other directories grow out of the root.

■ You can create and remove directories easily with the Shell.

■ You can view a directory listing many different ways.

■ Detailed information about the current file, directory, and disk are only a menu choice away.

In the next chapter, you will learn how to use E Editor, the built-in PC DOS 6 text processor.

6

Using the
E Editor

Nowadays, word processing software is becoming increasingly sophisticated. Application packages like Word or WordPerfect almost universally incorporate desktop publishing features such as page layout and font selection. If you only need to draft a letter or send a memo, you may not want to spend time learning about style sheets or printer files.

DOS 6 offers the E Editor, a new, full-screen text editor that allows you to create, edit, and print memos, letters, and some DOS files without wasting time on a lot of bells and whistles. Edlin, the old DOS line editor, is still available, if you prefer, but you will find that the E Editor's interface is easy to learn and use.

This chapter introduces you to the E Editor. You will learn the basics of starting the E Editor and using it to create and print a text file. Once you discover how simple the E Editor is, you can take time on your own to learn some of its other features, such as search and replace, line drawing, and performing calculations (and storing keystrokes as mini-macros).

This chapter is only an introduction to the E Editor. For more information, refer to the on-line Help feature or the *DOS User's Guide*.

Starting the E Editor

Creating a text file with the E Editor

Adding, deleting, and manipulating text with the E Editor.

Saving a file with the E Editor

Printing a file with the E Editor

Exiting the E Editor

Key Terms Used in This Chapter	
ASCII file	A file consisting of alphanumeric and control characters, which can be text or other information you can easily read. Control characters include Ctrl, Alt, and Esc.
E Editor command line	An area in the E Editor window where you can enter text editing commands. It appears directly above the E Editor status line, and directly below the main text area.
E Editor status line	An area in the E Editor window that displays information about the current file, including the filename, the numbers of the text line and column the cursor is on, and whether insert mode is on.
Function keys	The special command keys indicated on your keyboard by the letter F. Most keyboards have between ten and twelve function keys.

7

Starting the Editor

The E Editor creates and saves unformatted, or *ASCII*, text files. ASCII files contain only text characters and a few control characters you can enter on your keyboard, such as tabs and hard returns. You can use the E Editor to edit files that are not simple ASCII files, such as word processing files, however most word processing files contain special format and control information in addition to plain text. These files lose their formatting when you open the files with the E Editor.

To start the E Editor from the DOS Shell, follow these steps:

1. Open the Main program group, if it is not already open, by double-clicking Main in the program list, or by selecting Main and pressing Enter.

2. Double-click the PC DOS E Editor, or select it and press Enter. The File to Edit Dialog box appears. Or, choose **O**pen from the File menu. The File to Edit dialog box appears.

3. To start the E Editor without opening an existing file, choose OK. If you want to open an existing file, type the filename in the `File to edit?` text box and choose OK.

You do not have to enter a filename to start the E Editor. If you enter the name of an existing file, that file loads into the Editor and appears on your screen. The filename appears on the status line at the bottom of the screen. Be sure to enter the complete path to the file along with the filename.

If you do not enter a filename, the E Editor starts without an existing file. The status line indicates that the file is unnamed. If you enter the name of a new file in the `File to edit?` text box, the E Editor starts with no file loaded, but the status line at the bottom of the screen indicates the new filename.

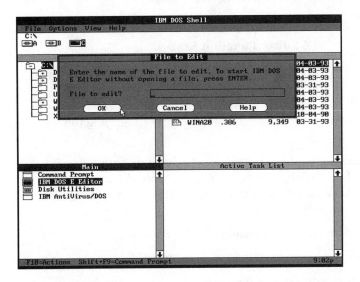

To start the E Editor from the Shell without opening a file, choose OK in the File to Edit Dialog box without entering a filename.

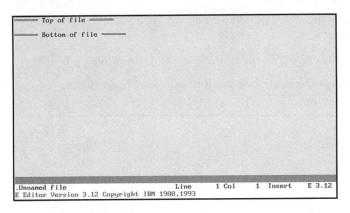

The status line near the bottom of the E Editor window indicates that the open file is unnamed.

The E Editor provides a full screen window for entering text. Characters that you type on your keyboard appear at the cursor location, between the Top of file and Bottom of file markers. The status line near the bottom of the screen that indicates the filename also displays the text line number, the column number, and whether insert mode is turned on. The line above the status line is the *E Editor command line.* You use the command line to perform basic tasks such as naming a file.

When you begin typing text, the actions associated with the *function keys* are displayed below the status line, in the function key text area. The function keys let you perform most E Editor tasks with only one keystroke. Press the Alt, Shift, or Ctrl key to display additional function keys. Table 7.1 lists the basic E Editor function keys and their associated actions.

Table 7.1
E Editor Function Keys

Key	Action
F1	Displays on-line Help.
F2	Saves the text file you are editing without quitting the E Editor.
F3	Quits the E Editor and returns to the Shell without saving the file. If changes have been made since the last save, the E Editor asks if you want to quit without saving. From the on-line Help, F3 returns to the E Editor.
F4	Saves the current file and quits the E Editor.
F6	Shows the options for drawing text graphics.
F7	Changes the current filename.
F8	Opens the specified file for editing, without closing the current file.
F9	Cancels editing changes made to the current line.
F10	Displays the next open file for editing without closing the current file.

7

Creating a Text File

To create a text file, simply type your text in the E Editor window. The E Editor does not have word wrap—you must press Enter to move the cursor to the next line. If you do not press Enter, the line of text scrolls to the left, which means that the characters at the beginning of the line disappear off the left side of the screen. Press the left arrow key or the home key to scroll back to the beginning of the line. A line of text in the E Editor can be up to 256 characters long.

You can use the cursor control keys to move around the file as you type, or to view parts of the file that have already been entered. Table 7.2 lists the cursor control keys and their functions.

Table 7.2
E Editor Cursor Control Keys

Key	*Action*
↑ ↓	Moves up/down one line.
← →	Moves left/right one character.
Home	Moves to column 1 of the current line.
End	Moves to the last character of the current line.
PgUp	Moves to the text up one page.
PgDn	Moves to the text down one page.
Ctrl-Home	Moves to the first line in the file.
Ctrl-End	Moves to the last line in the file.
Ctrl-PgUp	Moves to the first line of the current screen.
Ctrl-PgDn	Moves to the last line of the current screen.
Ctrl-←	Moves to the first character of the current word.
Ctrl-→	Moves to the last character of the current word.
Ctrl-↵Enter	Moves to column 1 of the next line.
Tab↹	Moves to the next tab stop.

continues

7

Table 7.2 *(Continued)*

Key	Action
⇧Shift-Tab⇄	Moves to the previous tab stop.
Esc	Moves the cursor between the text and command areas.
Del	Deletes the character at the cursor location.
←Backspace	Deletes the character to the left of the cursor.
Ctrl-←Backspace	Deletes the entire line of text the cursor is on.

Naming an Unnamed File

When you started the E Editor, you either opened a text file by typing the filename in the File to edit? text box, or you opened a new, unnamed file. Before you can save a file with the E Editor, the file must have a name.

To name a file, follow these steps:

1. Press F7, the name function key. The cursor moves down to the E Editor command line. The Name command is entered there.
2. Type the filename. Remember to include the complete path. If you do not include the complete path, the file will be saved in the current directory.
3. Press ↵Enter. The name appears under the command line.
4. Press Esc to move the cursor back to the text area.

You can also use the F7 function key to rename the file you are currently editing. Renaming the current file does not change the name of the previous version of the file stored on your disk. It lets you save a new version of the file with a new name. Follow the same procedure used for naming a new file. Press Esc to return to the text area and continue editing the file with its new name.

Editing with the E Editor

The PC DOS E Editor is a powerful line editor that contains many of the same features found in high-end word processors. With just one or two keystrokes you can perform most editing tasks, including inserting, deleting, moving, and copying blocks of text.

126

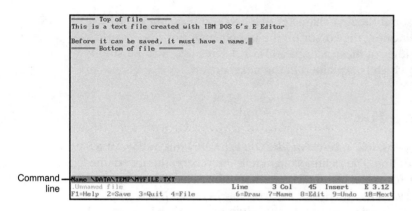

Command line

Press F7 and enter the complete path and filename on the E Editor command line. In this example, the file MYFILE.TXT will be stored in the \DATA\TEMP subdirectory.

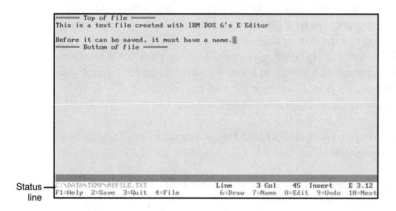

Status line

When you press Enter, the filename and path appear on the status line. Press Esc to move the cursor back to the text area.

Entering Text to a File

When you open the E Editor to a new file, you can immediately begin typing your new document. If you open the E Editor to an existing file, you can immediately begin making changes to the original file.

As mentioned earlier, the E Editor is a text line editor. Consequently, at the end of one line the E Editor does not automatically wrap text to the next line. If you keep typing beyond the end of your screen, the E Editor places all the text on one line—up to 256 characters—unless you have set margins. You must press Enter to insert *line breaks* or *line feeds* at the end of each line.

As you type your text, you should press Enter to add line feeds. If you go back later and try to break a line by pressing Enter, you'll see that a new line is inserted between the current line of text and the next line; the original line of text remains intact (unsplit). Likewise, you cannot remove a line feed by positioning the cursor at the first character of a line and pressing the Backspace key or by positioning the cursor on the last character of a line and pressing Delete. Neither of these actions adds or deletes text; you must follow a special sequence, which is explained in the next section.

Adding Text to a File

When the E Editor opens, it is in *Insert mode*. You can verify this by checking the right side of the status line. The rightmost item tells the version number of the E Editor, and the item just to the left of the version number identifies the editing mode: Insert or Replace. Press the Insert key to toggle between Insert and Replace. Notice that the cursor is block shaped when Insert mode is active and resembles an underline character when Replace mode is active. When you toggle to Insert mode, each character you type is inserted at the location of the cursor, and all the text to the right of the cursor shifts right one position. When you toggle to Replace mode, the text you type *replaces* the text at the cursor location. You'll probably want to leave the E Editor in Insert mode at all times. Even if you are replacing a line of text, it's easier to delete the old line after you've inserted the new, rather than risk accidentally overwriting valid text.

Sometimes you want to split a line of text into two separate lines. To split a line of text, follow these steps:

1. Place the cursor on the character you want as the first character of the new line.
2. Press [Alt]-[S]. The text from the cursor location to the end of the line is moved to the beginning of a new line that is inserted below the original. The cursor remains at its original location, which now is the end of the line.

Deleting Text from a File

You can remove text one character at a time, one word at a time, or one line at a time. To remove text one character at a time, use the Delete key, which removes text at the cursor location, or the Backspace key, which removes text to the left of the cursor.

To remove text one word at a time, follow these steps:

1. Place the cursor at the beginning of the word to be deleted.
2. Press [Ctrl]-[D]. The characters from the cursor position to the end of the word are deleted.

To remove an entire line of text, follow these steps:

1. Move the cursor to any location on the line you want to delete.
2. Press Ctrl-◆Backspace. The entire line is deleted and the text below the deleted line all moves up one line. The cursor remains in the same position, but on the new line.

Neither of the two preceding commands will delete a line feed or join two lines. To join two lines separated by a line feed, perform the following steps:

1. Place the cursor anywhere on the line you want to add to.
2. Press Alt-J. This command automatically moves the line below the cursor up to the end of the line on which the cursor is positioned. The E Editor inserts a space between the original text and the joined text.

By selecting and manipulating blocks of text, you can perform advanced editing functions on your text files.

Marking Text

You begin most advanced editing operations by *marking* (or *selecting*) a block of text. In a single line, you can mark any amount of text—from a single character to the entire line. You can also mark several lines or the entire file all at once.

The E Editor enables you to mark different sizes and shapes of text and then perform various functions, such as copying, moving, or deleting. When done correctly, the area you have marked is highlighted on your screen.

The following four types of marks are recognized in the E Editor:

Character	The single character on which the cursor is placed is marked.
Word	One word is marked.
Line	An entire line is marked, from column 1 up to and including column 255.
Block	A strictly rectangular block of text is marked.

To mark a character, follow these steps:

1. Use the arrow keys or other cursor-movement keys to move the cursor to the character you want to mark.
2. Press Alt-Z.

The E Editor defines a *word* as a string of characters beginning at the cursor position, up to and including the first following space. Unlike the line mark, which marks an entire line, you can mark only a single word with a word mark.

To mark a word, follow these steps:

1. Use the arrow keys or other cursor-movement keys to move the cursor anywhere in the word you want to mark.
2. Press Alt-W.

A *line* of text is any group of characters or words that appears on a single row between column 1 and the next line-feed character. To mark a line of text, follow these steps:

1. Use the arrow keys or other cursor-movement keys to move the cursor anywhere in the line you want to mark.
2. Press Alt-L.

A *block* of text is any group of characters, words, lines, or paragraphs of continuous text. You can mark a block of text by pressing Alt-L on consecutive lines, or you can perform the following steps:

1. Use the arrow keys or other cursor-movement keys to move the cursor to the upper, leftmost character of the text you want to mark.
2. Press Alt-B.
3. Move the cursor to the lower, rightmost character of the text you want to block mark. Press Alt-B again to highlight the entire block.

To unmark highlighted text, press Alt-U .

Copying Text

You use the Copy function to copy and reposition a block of text. This command is handy when you want to use a block of text in another location without affecting the original block of text.

To copy a block of text, perform the following steps:

1. Mark the block of text you want to copy.

   Refer to the preceding section on "Marking Text" if you need help with that task.
2. Mark the destination for the highlighted text by moving the cursor to the destination position.

3. Press [Alt]-[C].

   The block of text is copied to the new location but is not removed from its original location.

You might want to write letters to several different people that relay essentially the same information. You can use the Copy feature to insert marked text into multiple files and leave the original untouched.

To copy a block of text into another file, perform the following steps:

1. Load the files that you want to transfer text between.

2. In the file that has the text you want to copy, mark the block of text.

   Refer to the preceding section on "Marking Text" if you need help with that task.

3. Mark the destination for the highlighted text by switching to the second file ([F10]) and moving the cursor to the destination position.

4. Press [Alt]-[C].

   The block of text is copied to the new location and is not removed from its original location.

You can copy the marked text into a file as many times as necessary by repeating the Copy command ([Alt]-[C]). The text remains in the *buffer*, a temporary storage area, until you change what is marked.

Moving Text

If you want to rearrange the order of text in a file, you can move a block of text.

To move a block of text, perform the following steps:

1. Mark the block of text you want to move.

   Refer to the section on "Marking Text" that appeared earlier in this chapter if you need help with this task.

2. Mark the destination for the highlighted text by switching to the second file ([F10]) and moving the cursor to the destination position.

3. Press [Alt]-[M].

   The block of text is deleted from the original location and moved to the new destination.

7

To move a block of text into another file, perform the following steps:

1. Load the files that you want to transfer text between.

2. In the file that has the text you want to move, mark the block of text.

   Refer to the section on "Marking Text" earlier in this chapter if you need help with this task.

3. Mark the destination for the highlighted text by switching to the second file (F10) and moving the cursor to the destination position.

4. Press Alt-M.

   The block of text is moved to the new location and is removed from its original location.

When you choose the Move command, the text is not removed from the buffer but remains there until you move another block of text into the buffer. You can insert text from the buffer into a file as many times as you want by repeating the Move commands (Alt-M).

Saving a File

When you have completed entering or editing text, you must save the file. Actually, it is a good idea to save the file periodically, even while you are still working on it. If something happens to disrupt your computer session, you still have a copy of the file saved.

There are three ways to save a file with the E Editor:

- You can save the file and continue editing.
- You can save the file with a new name, or in a new directory, and continue editing.
- You can save the file and quit the E Editor.

No matter which method of saving that you use, notice that when you save, a message flashes in the function key area telling you that the file is being saved.

To save the file and continue editing, press F2. The file is saved in the current directory, or in the directory specified with the filename. You can continue editing the file.

Remember, the file must have a name before it can be saved. If you try to save an unnamed file, a File not found error message is displayed in the function key text area.

7

To save the file with a new name or in a new directory, press Esc to move the cursor to the E Editor command line. Type **SAVE** and then the new path and filename. The file will be saved in the new directory, or with the new name, but the original file is still displayed on your screen. Press Esc to move the cursor back to the text area to continue editing the original file.

To save the file and quit the E Editor, press F4. The file will be saved with its current name and path, and you will return to the DOS Shell.

Printing a File

You can use the E Editor to print the open file displayed on your screen. Before trying to print a file, make sure that your printer is turned on, loaded with paper, and correctly attached to the LPT1 port of your computer.

To print a file with the E Editor, follow these steps:

1. Start the E Editor and open the file you want to print. For example, if you want to print the file MYFILE.TXT that is stored in the \DATA\TEMP subdirectory, choose **O**pen from the File menu and type **\DATA\TEMP\MYFILE.TXT** in the File to edit? text box.
2. Press Esc to move the cursor to the E Editor command line.
3. Type **PRINT** and press Enter. The E Editor prints the file.
4. Press Esc to move the cursor back to the text area and continue editing the file.

The E Editor checks the printer before it prints. If the printer is not turned on, out of paper, or off-line, the E Editor displays the error message Printer not ready. Check your printer and try issuing the PRINT command again.

Exiting the Editor

When you have finished creating or editing text files, you can exit the E Editor and return to the DOS Shell. There are two ways to exit:

- Press F3 to quit. If you have made changes to any open file since the last time you saved it, the E Editor displays a message in the function key area asking if you want to quit without saving. Press Y to return to the DOS Shell without saving the changes. Press N to return to the current file.
- Press F4 to save all open files and return to the DOS Shell.

If you press F3 without first saving changes, the E Editor displays a message in the function key area asking if you want to Quit without saving?

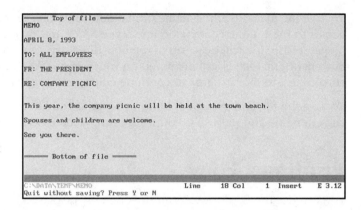

Lessons Learned

■ You can easily create, edit, and print text files with the E Editor.

■ Most tasks can be accomplished in the E Editor simply by pressing a function key.

■ You can save versions of the same file with different names or in different directories.

■ You can print the open file to a printer attached to your PC's LPT1 port.

In the next chapter, you learn about the DOS command line, and how to use the twenty most common DOS commands.

7

Command Line Essentials

Before PC DOS 5, you had to learn how to use the command line before you could put DOS to work. Now, because the Shell is so easy to use, you can learn the command line after you become familiar with using DOS and running programs.

The DOS command line, however, can be faster and more powerful than the Shell because it allows you more flexibility in selecting and starting commands. In this chapter you will learn to issue commands at the command line, and you will learn about twenty of the most common and useful DOS commands.

Moving from
the Shell to the
command line

Understanding
commands and
the command
line

Using DOSKey,
the command
line editor

The DOS top 20

Key Terms Used in This Chapter	
Command	Information that you type that tells the computer what you want to do. Most commands are representative of English words, with single numbers or letters often added as optional instructions.
Command line	The area on the screen where the cursor appears next to the DOS prompt. You can type DOS commands rather than using the Shell.
DOS prompt	An indicator, such as *C:\>*, that identifies the command line. You can issue DOS commands directly from the DOS prompt, as opposed to indirectly from the Shell.
Syntax	The specific structure you follow when you issue commands.
Parameter	Any additional information you type in addition to the command name to be more specific about what you want the DOS command to do.
Switch	A part of the command that turns on an optional instruction or function.
Delimiter	A character that separates the parts of a command. Common delimiters are the space and the slash (/).
Path	A DOS command parameter that tells DOS where to find a file or where to carry out a command.

8

Moving from the Shell to the Command Line

This book has covered a lot of territory already. You have learned about the structure of DOS, about disks and directories, and how to use the DOS Shell to perform the most important commands. You now know how to be fully productive with your personal computer and DOS—all accomplished without using the DOS command line.

So why bother with the command line now? There are a number of reasons:

- You cannot use all DOS commands from the Shell. Sometimes you must use the command line.

- You must know the command line to create batch files to customize your system.

- You sometimes used the command line from within the Shell without knowing it. When you complete the parameters in the dialog box for the Format command, for example, you are really using the command line. After you know more about using the command line, you will find that using the Shell is even easier.

Most of what you can do in the Shell you can do at the command line. Usually the Shell is much easier to use. At times, however, you will find that certain commands or command sequences run faster from the command line. When you know how to use both methods, you have more control over your personal computer.

As you learned in Chapter 4, you can get to the DOS command line from the Shell in two ways. You can quit the Shell and remove it from memory, or you can suspend it temporarily.

Before you quit the Shell, make sure that all active tasks in the Swapper have been closed. Then, do any one of the following:

- Press F3.
- Press Alt-F4.
- Choose Exit from the File menu.

To return to the Shell, type **DOSSHELL** at the command line and press Enter.

To suspend the Shell temporarily to use the command line, use one of the following:

- Press Shift-F9.
- Select the Command Prompt program from the program area.

To resume the Shell, type **EXIT** at the command line and press Enter. You return to the Shell, and all active tasks remain active.

Understanding Commands and the Command Line

When you use the *command line,* you use the *DOS prompt,* or the *command prompt.* All three terms mean exactly the same thing. When you see the

8

prompt on the command line you know that DOS is ready for your next command. You can change this prompt, using the PROMPT command explained later in this chapter.

The standard prompt that most people use with a hard disk displays the current drive and path. With this prompt, you always know the current directory. For example, the prompt C:\> indicates that drive C is the current drive and the root is the current directory.

To tell DOS what you want to do, you enter DOS *commands.* Commands are letters, numbers, and acronyms separated by certain other characters. Stripped of jargon, using a DOS command is like telling your dog to "sit," "heel," or "stay." Additionally, you can tell your computer to "sit and bark" concurrently. DOS commands frequently, though not exclusively, use slash marks (/) to indicate additional instructions.

A command you give to DOS is similar to a written instruction you might give to a work associate, but with DOS you must be precise. People use interconnecting words and inferences that the human brain can grasp easily. DOS knows only what its developers programmed it to understand.

When you type a command in its proper form—or *syntax*—at the DOS prompt, both the DOS command and any additional parameters communicate your intent. Both relay the action you want to perform and the object of that action. Remember, your main tool for communication with your PC is the keyboard. Your PC is ready to work for you, but it doesn't respond to humor, anger, frustration, or imprecise syntax.

Assume that you have an assistant with a limited vocabulary. If you want a sign on a bulletin board duplicated for posting on another bulletin board, you might instruct, "Copy sign A to sign B. Make sure that the copy is free from errors."

Similarly, if you want DOS to duplicate all the data from a diskette in drive A to a diskette you have placed in drive B, you give DOS the following instruction:

DISKCOPY A: B:

To have DOS, the efficient helper, compare the copy and the original to make sure that both diskettes contain exactly the same files and file sizes, type the following command:

DISKCOMP A: B:

DISKCOPY and DISKCOMP are good examples of DOS commands that are clearly named to explain the activity they perform. A: and B: indicate the diskette drives you want DOS to use.

8

Learning the ins and outs of issuing DOS commands takes practice. DOS commands follow a structure that is far more rigid than a casual conversation with an assistant. Some of this rigidity is masked when you use the Shell.

The strength of DOS shines through when you understand its rules; everything flows easily. Commands conform to standard rules in their command-line structure. DOS is easier to use when you understand the concepts behind the commands. You can then generalize rules to different commands. To feel comfortable with DOS commands, remember these rules:

- DOS requires you to use a specific set of rules, or syntax, when you issue commands.
- Parameters, part of a command's syntax, change the way DOS runs a command.

You can think of the command name as the action part of a DOS command. In addition to the name, many commands require or allow further directions. Any such directions are called *parameters.* A parameter is a specific instruction DOS must apply to the general action of the command. Using DOS commands is quite easy if you follow the rules of order and use the correct parameters.

Syntax

Syntax is the structure, order, and vocabulary in which you type the elements of the DOS command. Using proper syntax when you enter a DOS command is comparable to using proper English when you speak. To carry out your command, DOS must clearly understand what you are typing.

When you use the Shell, you do not have to know some of the syntax, because the information is built into the menus and program items. You do run into the rules of syntax, however, when you need to complete some dialog boxes. With the command line, you must know the syntax every time you use a command.

Many DOS manuals use *symbolic form* to describe command syntax. Simply stated, symbolic form is the use of a letter or name for illustrative purposes. A file used to illustrate a command might be called EXAMPLE.COM. Actually, EXAMPLE.COM exists only in the mind of the writer. It is an example. When you enter the real command, you are supposed to substitute a real name for the symbolic one.

A Command References normally lists every command switch (option), as though multiple switches are a normal part of the command. Many DOS

8

commands cannot be issued to accept every possible option. Using all the options is like ordering a sandwich with white, rye, whole wheat, *and* cinnamon-raisin bread. The choice is usually either/or, rather than all. A command should contain nothing more than what you want to instruct DOS to do.

Symbolic form is used to describe not only files, but also the entire command line. A DIR command shown in symbolic form might look like this:

DIR *d:path\ filename.ext* /W /P /A:*attributes* /O:*order* /S /B /L

On the other hand, a command that you would use in the real world might look like the following example:

DIR C: /W /P

As you can see, symbolic notation can confuse, rather than enlighten, until you understand the concept behind the form.

Switches

A *switch* is a parameter that turns on an optional function of a command. In the preceding DIR example, /W and /P are switches. Note that each switch is a slash followed by a character. Not all DOS commands use switches. In addition, switches may have different meanings for different commands.

You can use the /W switch with the DIR command to display a wide directory of files. Normally, DIR displays a directory with one file listing per line. The date and time the file was created are displayed next to the filename. As the screen fills, the first files scroll off the top of the display. The /W switch displays a directory listing that shows only filenames and extensions and displays them in multiple columns across the screen.

Sometimes a directory contains too many files to display on one screen. When you use the /P switch with the directory command, 23 lines of filenames— approximately one full screen—are displayed. The display pauses when the screen fills. At the bottom of a paused directory listing, DOS prompts you to Press any key to continue to move to the next screen of files. The /P switch thus enables you to see all the files in the directory, one screen at a time.

When DOS says Press any key to continue, you can press *almost* any key. If you press the Shift, Alt, Caps Lock, Num Lock, or Scroll Lock keys, DOS ignores you. The easiest keys to press are the space bar and the Enter key.

Many DOS commands can be typed in several forms and still be correct. Although the simple versions of DOS syntax work effectively, most DOS manuals show the complete syntax for a command, which can be confusing.

8

140

Issuing Commands

The command name is a key to DOS. The command processor, COMMAND.COM, reads the command you type. COMMAND.COM can carry out several "built in," or internal, commands. It also knows how to load and run the external utility programs you enter at the DOS prompt. In the Shell, you choose a command from a menu or a list of programs in a group. At the command line, you type the command name.

Typing the Command Name

When you type a command, do not leave a space after the DOS prompt's greater-than sign (>). Enter the command name directly after the prompt. If the command has no parameters or switches, press the Enter key after the last letter of the command name. For example, you type the directory command as **DIR** at the prompt and then press Enter.

Adding Parameters

Parameters that are not switches appear in this book in two ways: lowercase and uppercase. You must supply the value for the lowercase text. The lowercase letters are shorthand for the full names of the parts of a command. When you read *filename.ext*, you are supposed to type the name of the actual file. Uppercase means that you enter letter-for-letter what you see.

Remember that you separate parameters from the rest of the command. Most of the time the delimiter is a space, but other delimiters exist, such as the comma (,), the backslash (\), and the colon (:). Just look at the examples in this book to learn the correct delimiter.

If the example command has switches, you can recognize them by the preceding slash (/). Always enter the switch letter exactly as shown in this book. Remember to type the slash.

Ignoring a Command (Esc)

Don't worry if you mistype a command. Until you press Enter, DOS does not act on the command. You can correct a mistake by using the arrow keys or the Backspace key to reposition the cursor. Press Esc if you want to start again from the beginning. The Esc key withdraws the entry and gives you a new line.

8

141

Just remember that these line-editing and canceling tips work only before you press the Enter key. Some commands can be successfully stopped with the Ctrl-C or Ctrl-Break sequence, but checking that the command is typed correctly before you press Enter is always a good practice.

Starting a Command

The Enter key is the action key for DOS commands. Make it a habit to pause and read what you have typed before you press Enter. After you press Enter, the computer carries out your command. During the processing of the command, DOS does not display any keystrokes you might type, but it does remember them and may display them as soon as it is done running the current command.

Using DOS Editing Keys

When you type a command and press the Enter key, DOS copies the command into an input *buffer,* a storage area for commands. You can retrieve the last command from the buffer and use it again. This feature is helpful when you want to issue a command that is similar to your last command. Table 8.1 lists the keys you use to edit the input buffer.

Table 8.1
DOS Command Line Editing Keys

Key	*Action*
Tab	Moves cursor to the next tab stop.
Esc	Cancels the current line and does not change the buffer.
Ins	Enables you to insert characters in the line.
Del	Deletes a character from the line.
F1 or ←Backspace	Copies one character from the preceding command line.
F2	Copies all characters from the preceding command line up to the next character you type.
F3	Copies all remaining characters from the preceding command line.

142

Key	Action
F4	Deletes all characters from the preceding command line up to, but not including, the next character typed (opposite of F2).
F5	Moves the current line into the buffer, but does not allow DOS to execute the line.
F6	Produces an end-of-file marker when you copy from the console to a disk file.

Controlling Scrolling

Scrolling describes the way in which a screen fills with information; the lines of the display "scroll off" the top of the screen as the screen fills with information. To stop a scrolling screen, press the key combination Ctrl-S. Press any key to restart the scrolling. On enhanced keyboards, you can press the Pause key to stop the scrolling.

Using DOSKey, the Command Line Editor

The DOS Shell is the best way to learn how to use DOS commands. After you are familiar with the common DOS commands, you may find yourself using the command line more often. When you use the command line, you find that you repeat many commands over and over, sometimes with slight variations. With the command line editor, DOSKey, you can retrieve previous commands without retyping them. At times, you may type a long command and make an error. Whether you catch the error before or after you press Enter, you can correct the error without retyping the entire command.

DOSKey is not built into COMMAND.COM. Before you can use DOSKey's features, you must load it into memory. At the prompt, type **DOSKEY** and press Enter. DOS responds with the message DOSKey installed.

DOSKey is installed and you can recall the command without retyping it. Now every time you enter a new command, DOSKey deletes the oldest command.

You need to enter the DOSKEY command only once per session.

8

Recalling Previous Commands with DOSKey

When DOSKey is loaded, to recall the last command entered, press the up-arrow key. To recall an earlier command, continue to press the up-arrow key until DOS displays the command you want. If you press the up-arrow key too many times and go past the command you want, press the down-arrow key to recall the next command in the buffer. To clear the command line so that you can enter a command from scratch, press the Esc key.

Suppose, for example, that you entered the following commands:

        C:
        CD\DATA\TAXES
        FORMAT A: /Q
        COPY *.* A:

These commands make the DATA\TAXES directory the current directory, quick format a diskette in drive A, and then copy all the files from the DATA\TAXES directory to the diskette in drive A.

When the copy procedure is complete, DOS displays the DOS prompt. If you want to repeat this process for the DATA\FIGURES directory, you can retype each command or use DOSKey to recall the previous commands without retyping them.

When you press the up-arrow key once, you recall the last command entered: COPY *.* A:.

```
QuickFormatting 1.2M
Format complete.

Volume label (11 characters, ENTER for none)?

    1213952 bytes total disk space
    1213952 bytes available on disk

       512 bytes in each allocation unit.
      2371 allocation units available on disk.

Volume Serial Number is 3E17-15D0

QuickFormat another (Y/N)?n

C:\DATA\TAXES>COPY *.* A:
CHECKS.WK1
INCOME.WK1
LOG.DOC
STATEMNT.WK1
TAXEST.WK1
        5 file(s) copied

C:\DATA\TAXES>COPY *.* A:
```

8

```
QuickFormatting 1.2M
Format complete.

Volume label (11 characters, ENTER for none)?

   1213952 bytes total disk space
   1213952 bytes available on disk

       512 bytes in each allocation unit.
      2371 allocation units available on disk.

Volume Serial Number is 3E17-1500

QuickFormat another (Y/N)?n

C:\DATA\TAXES>COPY *.* A:
CHECKS.WK1
INCOME.WK1
LOG.DOC
STATEMNT.WK1
TAXEST.WK1
        5 file(s) copied

C:\DATA\TAXES>CD\DATA\TAXES
```

When you press the up-arrow key two more times, you recall the third-from-the-last command entered: CD\DATA\TAXES.

After you recall a previous command, you can press Enter to execute it again, or you can edit or change the command before you execute it. If you recall the command CD\DATA\TAXES and want to change it to CD\DATA\FIGURES, press the Backspace key five times to erase the word *TAXES*. Then type **FIGURES** and press Enter.

```
Volume label (11 characters, ENTER for none)?

   1213952 bytes total disk space
   1213952 bytes available on disk

       512 bytes in each allocation unit.
      2371 allocation units available on disk.

Volume Serial Number is 3E17-1500

QuickFormat another (Y/N)?n

C:\DATA\TAXES>COPY *.* A:
CHECKS.WK1
INCOME.WK1
LOG.DOC
STATEMNT.WK1
TAXEST.WK1
        5 file(s) copied

C:\DATA\TAXES>CD\DATA\FIGURES

C:\DATA\FIGURES>
```

The recalled command is CD\DATA\TAXES. The edited command makes DATA\FIGURES the current directory.

8

145

Table 8.2 lists keys you can use with DOSKey to recall commands.

Table 8.2
Keys To Recall Previous Commands

Key	Action
↓	Recalls the previous command.
↑	Recalls the next command.
Esc	Clears the command line.
PgUp	Recalls the oldest command.
PgDn	Recalls the most recent command.
F7	Lists all commands in the buffer.

Editing Previous Commands with DOSKey

After you recall a command, you can edit the command before you run it
again. You already learned to use the Backspace key to erase characters at the
end of the command. DOSKey also provides a line editor that enables you to
change any part of the command. Table 8.3 lists all the DOSKey editing keys.
Editing a command is similar to editing a line of text with the DOS Editor
or a word processing program. The only difference is that you can edit only
one line.

Suppose, for example, that you start the following command:

COPY *.DOC D:\BACKUP

You also want to copy all the files with a WK1 extension to the D:\BACKUP
directory. Follow these steps:

1. Press ↓ once to recall the COPY command.
2. Press Home to move the cursor to the beginning of the command line.
3. Press ← seven times to move the cursor to the D in DOC.
4. Type **WK1** in place of DOC.
5. Press ↵Enter.

8

146

Table 8.3
DOSKey Editing Keys

Key	Action
[Home]	Moves the cursor to the beginning of the command.
[End]	Moves the cursor to the end of the command.
[→]	Moves the cursor one character to the left.
[←]	Moves the cursor one character to the right.
[Ctrl]-[←]	Moves the cursor one word to the left.
[Ctrl]-[→]	Moves the cursor one word to the right.
[←Backspace]	Deletes one character to the left of the cursor.
[Del]	Deletes one character at the cursor position.
[Ctrl]-[End]	Deletes all characters from the cursor to the end of the command.
[Ctrl]-[Home]	Deletes all characters from the cursor to the beginning of the command.
[Ins]	Toggles between Overtype and Insert modes. In Overtype mode, everything you type replaces existing characters. In Insert mode, the cursor changes from an underline to a square block, and everything you type is inserted at the cursor.
[Esc]	Clears the command line.

DOSKey has other features that are beyond the scope of this book.

The DOS Top 20

Although you may never use more than ten commands, DOS recognizes and responds to dozens of them. Use this section to familiarize yourself with twenty of the most common and useful DOS commands.

- The entry then explains the command's purpose and shows the syntax required to invoke the command. In the syntax, *d:* is the name of the disk drive holding the file, and *path* is the directory path to the file.

8

filename is the name of the file, and *.ext* is the filename extension. Commands that use source and destination drive parameters use *sd:* for the source drive name and *dd:* for the destination drive name.

If any part of this notation does not appear in the syntax for the command, do not include the omitted part in the command.

- Next are step-by-step instructions for using the command.
- Last are any cautions, tips, or notes about the command, often including a brief comment indicating the emphasis you should place on mastering the command.

CHDIR or CD

Use CHDIR or CD to do the following:

- Change the current directory.
- Show the name of the current directory.

To use CHDIR or CD, follow these steps:

1. Type **CHDIR** or **CD**. CHDIR (CD) is an internal command that does not require a path.
2. Press the **space bar** once.
3. Type the drive name of the disk whose current directory you want to change (for example, **A:**, **B:**, or **C:**) and the name of the directory to which you want to change. If you don't specify a path, DOS displays the current path. Remember to use the backslash to separate the parts of the path.
4. Press ⏎Enter.

CHDIR is very important and simple to use; it is one of the commands you need so that you can navigate around your disk.

CHKDSK

Use CHKDSK to do the following:

- Checks the directory of the disk for disk and memory status. CHKDSK can display the following information:

    the number of files and directories on a disk

    the bytes used and the space available on a disk

    the presence of hidden files

8

       whether a diskette is bootable

       the total RAM and available RAM

       whether files are fragmented

- Makes minor repairs.

To use CHKDSK, follow these steps:

1. Type **CHKDSK** and press the **space bar** once. You might need to precede the command with the drive and path, because CHKDSK is an external command.

2. To check a disk on another drive, type the drive name, followed by a colon (:), after CHKDSK. For example, if your default drive is C and you want to check drive B, type **CHKDSK B:**.

3. You can use CHKDSK to determine the fragmented areas in an individual file by entering the path, filename, and extension. The filename and extension can contain wildcards.

4. Press ⏎Enter.

CHKDSK gives you more control of your computer. This simple command provides a quick analysis of your diskettes and hard disks. You should use it once a week.

COPY

Use COPY to do the following:

- Copy one or more files to another disk or directory, or copy a file to the same directory and change its name.
- Transfer information between DOS system devices.
- Send text to the printer.
- Create ASCII text files and batch files.

To use COPY, follow these steps:

1. Type **COPY** and press the **space bar** once.
2. Type the drive name and path of the source file (*sd:\spath*).
3. Type the name of the file you want to copy. You can use wildcards.
4. Press the **space bar**.
5. Type the drive name, path, and filename of the target file (*dd:\dpath*). Skip this step if the filename is to remain the same as that of the source file.

8

6. You also can add the /V switch to verify and check the accuracy of the COPY procedure

7. Press ⏎Enter.

Caution: Before you use this command, make sure that you have planned well. When you copy to another directory or disk, COPY overwrites a file of the same name, so be sure to type the filenames exactly, including directory names.

DATE

Use DATE to do the following:

- Enter or change the system date.
- Set the internal clock on a computer with a battery-backed clock.
- Check the current date stamp for newly created and modified files.
- Provide control for programs that require date information.

To use DATE, follow these steps:

1. Type **DATE** and press the **space bar** once.

2. Enter the date in the following format:

    mm-dd-yy (for North America; this format is the default)

    mm is a one- or two-digit number for the month (1 to 12).

    dd is a one- or two-digit number for the day (1 to 31).

    yy is a one- or two-digit number for the year (80 to 99). DOS assumes that the first two digits of the year are 19.

    You can separate the entries with hyphens, periods, or slashes.

3. Press ⏎Enter.

If your PC doesn't have a built-in calendar clock, use this command every time you boot. Knowing when files were written or updated is good organizational strategy and aids you in being selective with CPBACKUP and XCOPY. Better still, computers that contain battery-operated calendar clocks have become very inexpensive; you can purchase such a clock to eliminate typing the time and date every time you start your computer.

8

DEL or ERASE

Use DEL or ERASE to do the following:

- Remove one or more files from the current disk or directory.

To use DATE or ERASE, follow these steps:

1. Type **DEL** or **ERASE** and press the **space bar** once.
2. Type the drive name and path of the file you want to delete, unless the file is in the current directory.
3. Type the name of the file you want to delete.
4. You can use the following switch:

   /P prompts *filename* Delete (Y/N)? before each file is deleted. Press Y to delete the file or N to cancel the command.
5. Press Enter.

Caution: ERASE (DEL) is a deceptively simple command that can make your life easy or fill it with grief. Practice using this command and think carefully before pressing the Enter key. Be very careful when you use wildcards, or you might delete more files than you intend.

DIR

Use DIR to do the following:

- Display a list of files and subdirectories in a disk's directory.
- List a specified group of files within a directory.
- Examine the volume identification label of the disk.
- Determine the amount of available space on the disk.
- Check the size of individual files.
- Check the date the files were last modified.

To use DIR, follow these steps:

1. Type **DIR** and press the **space bar** once.
2. You also can type one of the following:

   The drive name of the directory you want to display.

   The path name of the directory you want to display.

   The filename, if you want to limit the number and types of files listed. You can use wildcards to list groups of files.

8

151

3. You can use any of the following switches:

   /W displays the directory in a wide format of five columns across. The /W switch displays only the directory name and filenames. For large listings, also include the /P switch.

   /P displays the directory and pauses between screen pages. This switch prevents large directories from scrolling off the screen before you can read them.

4. Press ⏎Enter.

DISKCOPY

Use DISKCOPY to do the following:

- Secure data against loss by duplicating a diskette. Note that DISKCOPY works only when copying diskettes of the same size and capacity.

To use DISKCOPY, follow these steps:

1. Type **DISKCOPY** and press the **space bar** once.
2. Type the name of the drive that holds the source (original) diskette (**A:**, for example). Press the **space bar** again.
3. Type the name of the drive that holds the target (new) diskette (**B:**, for example).
4. Press ⏎Enter. Within a few seconds, DOS prompts you to place the source diskette into drive A and the target diskette into drive B. If you have only one diskette drive, DOS prompts you to place the source diskette in drive A.
5. Insert the requested diskettes and press ⏎Enter. If you have only one diskette drive, DOS prompts you to exchange the source diskette with the target diskette.
6. When the copy is complete, DOS asks whether you want to copy another diskette.
7. Press Ⓨ and repeat steps 6 through 8 to copy another diskette; otherwise, press Ⓝ.

Tip: DISKCOPY is for duplicating diskettes, not hard disks. If a problem exists on the original (source) diskette, the same problem will appear on the duplicate diskette.

8

DOSSHELL

Use DOSSHELL to do the following:

- Perform DOS commands from menus.
- Manage files and directories.
- Manage and start programs.

To use DOSSHELL, follow these steps:

1. Type DOSSHELL. You might need to precede the command with the drive and path for DOSSHELL.COM because DOSSHELL is an external command.

2. Press ⏎Enter.

FORMAT

Use FORMAT to do the following:

- Prepare a diskette or hard disk to accept DOS information and files.

To use FORMAT, follow these steps:

1. Type **FORMAT**. You might need to precede the command with the drive and path if FORMAT is not in the root directory or in a path governed by the PATH command.

2. Press the **space bar** once.

   Note: You can use the /f switch to specify the capacity of a diskette. Type **/F:*size*** formats a diskette to a specific capacity, where *size* is one of the following diskette capacity values: 160, 180, 320, 360, 720, 1.2, 1.44, or 2.88.

3. Press ⏎Enter.

4. DOS now instructs you to place a diskette into the drive you specified. Insert the diskette you want to format and press ⏎Enter.

   In a few minutes, you see the message Format complete and a status report of the formatted disk.

   DOS then asks whether you want to format another disk.

5. Press Y and repeat steps 6 and 7 to format another disk; otherwise, press N.

8

Caution: If you format a 360K diskette in a 1.2M disk drive, the formatted disk might not be readable in a 360K drive. Also, a 1.2M disk might look exactly like a 360K diskette, but you cannot use the higher density 1.2M diskette in a 360K disk drive.

FORMAT is an absolute must to understand. This command is the heart of your disk maintenance system. If you accidentally format an already formatted disk, you may be able to recover the information by using the UNFORMAT command.

HELP

Use HELP to do the following:

- Display syntax for a command.

To use HELP, follow these steps:

1. Type **HELP** and press the **space bar** once. You might need to precede the command with the drive and path for HELP.EXE because HELP is an external command.
2. Type the command for which you want to get help (for example, FORMAT). If you do not enter a command name, HELP displays a complete listing of all the commands with a brief description of each.
3. Press ⏎Enter.

MKDIR or MD

Use MKDIR to do the following:

- Create subdirectories to help organize your files.

To use MKDIR or MD, follow these steps:

1. Type **MKDIR** or **MD** and press the **space bar** once.
2. If necessary, type the drive name and path of the new directory.
3. Type the directory name.
4. Press ⏎Enter.

If you have a hard disk drive, you need to understand this command.

MORE

Use MORE to do the following:

- Display data one screen at a time.

To use MORE, follow these steps:

1. Type the name of the file you want to display one full screen (23 lines) at a time, and press the **space bar** once. You may need to precede the syntax with a program name that acts on the filename.

2. Type **TYPE** *filename.ext* ¦ **MORE** and press the **space bar**.

3. Press ⏎Enter.

   The displayed information pauses when the screen is filled, DOS then displays the message - -More- -.

4. Press any key to display the next 23 lines of data.

MORE is very convenient for reading files longer than one screen.

PATH

Use PATH to do the following:

- Access files not in the default directory without changing directories. PATH tells DOS to search specified directories on specified drives if it does not find a program or batch file in the current directory.

To use PATH, follow these steps:

1. Type **PATH** and press the **space bar** once.

2. Type the drive name you want to include in the search path (for example, **A:**, **B:**, or **C:**). If you include the drive name with the path, DOS finds your files even if you change default drives.

3. Type the directory path you want to search (for example, **\KEEP**).

4. To add another directory to the search path, type a semicolon (;), and then type the drive name and path of the additional directory.

5. Repeat steps 2 through 4 until you type all the subdirectory paths you want DOS to search.

6. Press ⏎Enter.

PATH is an important navigational aid you should understand fully. If you don't understand PATH, you don't understand the directory concept.

8

PRINT

Use PRINT to do the following:

- Print a text file while you are using other IBM DOS commands.
- Display the contents of the print queue.

To use PRINT, follow these steps:

1. Type **PRINT** and press the **space bar**. You might need to precede the command with the drive and path if PRINT is not in the current directory or in a path governed by the PATH command.
2. Type the drive, path and filename of the file you want to print.
3. You can use any of the following switches:

    /C cancels printing of the preceding filename and subsequent filenames.

    /P adds the preceding filename and subsequent filenames to the print queue.
4. Press ⏎Enter.

Tip: Use PRINT without parameters to display the contents of the print queue.

PROMPT

Use PROMPT to do the following:

- Customize the DOS system prompt.
- Display the drive and directory path.
- Display a message on the computer.
- Display the date and time or the DOS version number.

To use PROMPT, follow these steps:

1. Type **PROMPT** and press the **space bar** once.
2. Type the text string and the arrangement of parameters you want to display.
3. You can use the following characters, preceded by $, with the PROMPT command to produce your own DOS prompt:

    $D displays the current date.

    $G displays the > character.

    $N displays the current disk drive name.

8

$P displays the current drive and path.

$T displays the system time.

PROMPT is used most frequently to extend the visual command line to display the path of your current directory.

RMDIR or RD

Use RMDIR to do the following:

* Remove a directory.

To use RMDIR or RD, follow these steps:

1. Use the ERASE command to delete all files from the directory you want to remove. Change to the parent directory of the directory you want removed.
2. Type **RMDIR** or **RD** and press the space bar once.
3. Type the drive name of the directory you want to remove.
4. Type the full path and name of the directory you want to remove.
5. Press ⏎Enter.

RMDIR is another essential command for maintaining a logical hard disk drive subdirectory system.

RENAME or REN

Use RENAME to do the following:

* Change the name of a file or group of files.

To use RENAME or REN, follow these steps:

1. Type **RENAME** or **REN** and press the **space bar** once.
2. Type the drive name and path of the file you want to rename.
3. Type the name of the file you want to rename. You can use wildcards (* and ?) to specify groups of files.
4. Press the **space bar**.
5. Type the new name you want to assign the file and press ⏎Enter.

Caution: Avoid giving files in different directories the same filename. You might accidentally delete the wrong file.

Practice this command to benefit from it fully.

8

TIME

Use TIME to do the following:

- Enter or change the time used by the computer.
- Set the automatic clock on a computer with a battery-backup clock.
- Establish the time that files were created or modified.
- Provide control for programs that require time information, like CPBACKUP and DOS ANTIVIRUS.

To use TIME, follow these steps:

1. Type **TIME** and press the **space bar** once.
2. Enter the time in the format *hh:mm:ss:xx* or *hh.mm.ss.xx*.

   For *hh*, type the hour, using one or two digits from 0 to 23. For *mm*, type the number of minutes, using one or two digits from 0 to 59. For *ss*, type the number of seconds, using one or two digits from 0 to 59. For *xx*, type the number of hundredths of a second, using one or two digits from 0 to 99. It is not necessary to include more than the hour and the minutes.
3. If you use the 12-hour clock when you enter the time, type **A** to represent AM hours or **P** to represent PM hours. For the 24-hour clock, omit these identifiers. (For example, to indicate 3:13 PM, type **3:13P** for the 12-hour clock or **15:13** for the 24-hour clock.)
4. Press 〔⏎Enter〕.

Use TIME with the DATE command. Including the correct time in a file may not be as important as including the date, but don't get into poor management habits. Better still, think about getting a battery-powered clock card for your PC to save time.

8

TYPE

Use TYPE to do the following:

- Display the contents of a text file on-screen.
- Send files to the printer.

To use TYPE, follow these steps:

1. Type **TYPE** and press the **space bar** once.
2. Type the drive name, path, and filename of the file you want to display.
3. Press ⏎Enter.

To send the typed output to a device such as the printer (PRN), use the redirection symbol >, as shown in this example: TYPE TEXT.TXT > PRN.

TYPE enables you to read a file without opening it in a word processing program.

XCOPY

Use XCOPY to do the following:

- Copy files from multiple directories to another disk.
- Copy files with a specific date.
- Copy newly created or modified files.
- Copy subdirectories and files.

To use XCOPY, follow these steps:

1. Type **XCOPY** and press the **space bar** once. You might need to precede the command with the drive and path for XCOPY.EXE because XCOPY is an external command.
2. Type the drive name and path of the source file (*sd:\spath*).
3. Type the name of the file you want to copy. You can use wildcards.
4. Press the **space bar**.
5. Type the drive name, path, and filename of the target file (*dd:\dpath\dfilename.ext*). Skip this step if the filename is to remain the same as that of the source file.
6. Press ⏎Enter.

Caution: Before you use XCOPY, make sure that you have typed the correct information so that you do not accidentally copy over important files.

Index